The Making of a Christian Mind

A Christian World View
& the Academic Enterprise

edited by
Arthur Holmes

INTERVARSITY PRESS
DOWNERS GROVE, ILLINOIS 60515

InterVarsity Press is the book-publishing division of Inter-Varsity Christian Fellowship, a student movement active on campus at hundreds of universities, colleges and schools of nursing. For information about local and regional activities, write IVCF, 233 Langdon St., Madison, WI 53703.

Distributed in Canada through InterVarsity Press, 860 Denison St., Unit 3, Markham, Ontario L3R 4H1, Canada.

Cover illustration: Roberta Polfus

ISBN 0-87784-525-5

Printed in the United States of America

Library of Congress Cataloging in Publication Data
Main entry under title:

The making of a Christian mind.

Bibliography: p.
    1. Christianity—Philosophy—Addresses, essays,
lectures.   2. Church and college—Addresses, essays,
lectures.   I. Holmes, Arthur Frank, 1924-
BR100.M266   1984 5   261.5   84-22476
ISBN 0-87784-525-5

16	15	14	13	12	11	10	9	8	7	6	5	4	3	2
97	96	95	94	93	92	91	90	89	88	87	86	85		

Foreword

Christian students have not always been blessed with the bright light now being shed by Christian scholars on academic disciplines from physics to philosophy, literature to life science. As I was doing doctoral studies in English some twenty years ago, I could find very few examples (in scholarly journals or the popular press) of Christians thinking Christianly about either my field or most others.

Thanks to Arthur Holmes, who then sponsored an annual philosophy conference at Wheaton College (and still does), I learned of some evangelical Christians who were doing their research within a Christian world view. Thanks to Jay Adams, who set me reading the work of a previous generation of scholars such as Abraham Kuyper and James Orr, I found that there has been a steady, though narrow, beam of light from the perspective of Reformed theology. And, finally, thanks to two graduate schools where the work of brilliant Catholic thinkers such as Etienne Gilson and Jacques Maritain had not been obscured by secular darkness, I began to see something of how the Christian faith illuminates all of life including the artistic, the rational and the academic.

In twenty years much has changed—changed for the better. In almost every area of intellectual endeavor, evangelical Christians are making a mark. Now undergraduate and graduate students who want to bring their studies under the lordship of Christ have many places to turn for help.

Perhaps the most fruitful of approaches to the integration of academic work and the Christian faith involves the analysis of world views. Here attention is drawn to the foundations on which all scholarly reflection is based. To know that the hard sciences developed out of a Christian notion of reality (a cosmos created by an orderly, rational, intentional, personal God) and that historically, modern sociology stems from naturalistic roots (the assumption that the cosmos is all there really is; there is no deity) is to begin to see why our task as Christians may be different in different academic disciplines. To understand that human beings are created in God's image is to see that no purely natural science will finally explain them. In fact, it may seriously distort our self-understanding.

With world-view analysis we have a valuable academic tool whose usefulness extends beyond the marketplace of ideas to the marketplace of life. In this book five Wheaton College scholars explain what a world view is, show how Christians in the past have developed ones for their age, illustrate how the Christian world view sheds light on our common natural and human reality and demonstrate how world-view analysis can act as a critical tool in evaluating modern theories of human nature. This book will be a stimulus to today's young minds to better the work of their teachers and their teachers' teachers. In every way, we today stand on the shoulders of yesterday's giants. What a pleasure to commend the shoulders of these five scholars to today's college women and men!

James W. Sire
Editor
InterVarsity Press

Preface

Education shapes lives. That is not its advertised purpose, but an inevitable result. The combined influences of required assignments, lectures and directed discussion, curricular design, the ethos of effective professors and even the general campus environment shape students' thoughts and lifestyles.

Decisions are mirrors of the soul, and souls are honed and shaped by the flow of information and the rub of other minds. Our decisions, when not based primarily on impulse, peer pressure or custom, normally rest on gathered data that has been filtered through the values and presuppositions that we hold. For a college or university student, where to look for data and how to interpret data are to a fair extent determined by educational experiences.

What does the Christian professor and the Christian liberal arts college have to offer? In our better moments we offer a transcending dynamic that relates all learning to biblical truth. This is not to claim that the Bible has the answers for every question or even the essential principles for every academic discipline. Rather it is a claim—even a commitment—that the biblical presentation of God as Creator of all, Communicator of truth, Redeemer of lives and the Convener of history lays a foundation of profound significance for understanding and decision making.

Wheaton College is a liberal arts college with such a commitment. Its Christian professors seek to integrate their knowledge of God and his Word with both their academic disciplines and their lives. While this is a continuing process, there are also times when it is fitting that we reaffirm our distinctive mission and renew our perspectives. Our 125th anniversary is just such an occasion for Wheaton College. Among the events of our celebrating year, we presented a series of chapel addresses on a Christian world view. This book is a record of those presentations.

The insights offered here by several of our faculty are propositions which distinguish this Christian college. Rarely will they be heard in the classrooms of secular colleges or universities. Yet there are many Christian students on these secular campuses who earnestly desire guidance for relating their personal faith to their present academic experiences. This collection, therefore, is intended to offer that assistance.

We commend this volume to Christian students everywhere for the personal enrichment and spiritual growth that comes from comprehending God as the Author of all truth.

J. Richard Chase, President
Wheaton College
January 1985

1
Toward a Christian View of Things

Arthur F. Holmes

How to order the mind on sound Christian principles at the very heart of where it is formed and informed, namely in the universities, is one of the two greatest themes that can be considered. . . . The problem is not only to win souls but to save minds. If you win the whole world and lose the mind of the world, you will soon discover you have not won the world. Indeed it may turn out that you have actually lost the world.[1]

These words of Charles Malik, Christian philosopher and former president of the United Nations, present Christians in academia with a strategic imperative for our day. To capture for Christ the modern mind, its attitudes and ideas concerning science, the arts and society, is both integral to the biblical mandate and crucial to future history. Nor is any individual conversion complete until a Christian mind is formed within. To bring our every thought into captivity to Christ, to think Christianly, to see all of life in relationship to the Creator and Lord of all, this is not an optional appendage of secondary importance, but is at the very heart of what it means to be Christian.

Christians in the World of Thought
Thinking Christianly means developing a Christian world view, and this is a creative, constructive task. Persuasive as a Christian world

view may prove to others, it is not primarily an apologetic defense of Christianity; and much as it may stand in contrast to non-Christian world views, it is not primarily a polemic against other positions. Rather it works out ways in which biblical beliefs and values can guide constructive thought and action. It explores the relationship of Christian faith to the various areas of human learning, interpreting the findings of science in a theistic context and valuing both scientific and artistic enterprises as God's good gifts. It brings biblical concepts of justice and love to the moral and social concerns of our time. By seeing everything in relation to the Creator-God incarnated in Jesus Christ, it gives unified meaning, direction and hope to all we do.

But of course other world views are at work in our world today, and history displays a variety of competing outlooks. Three major traditions stand out in both the past and now. From the time of the early Greeks to the present day, philosophical naturalism has sought to explain everything in terms of physical elements and processes. It gained momentum in the scientific revolution of the Renaissance and again in the last century and a half, giving rise to the scientific and technological mentality that now governs much of the Western approach to life's problems, and to Marxist ideologies the world over.

Parallel to this is a pantheistic tradition, nurtured by Neo-Platonic influences and by Eastern religions. Here the tendency is to subordinate the individual to the whole, to blur distinctions between moral good and evil, and perhaps to romanticize about the divinity in us all and the sacredness of all living things.

Yet a strong theistic tradition has been present in addition to the naturalistic and the pantheistic. Nurtured by the major theistic religions (Islam, Judaism and Christianity), emphasizing the sovereignty of the Creator-God and, especially in the Judeo-Christian tradition, his insistence on compassionate love and equal justice for even the lowliest of people, this theistic tradition has contributed immensely to the shape of philosophy in the West, and to art and to our social institutions.

This should come as no surprise once we recognize the breadth of concern in biblical religion. The Old Testament, its law and poets and prophets alike, addresses economic and political matters as well as personal religion and morality. It takes a lively interest in the intricate wonders of nature, the significance of historical events and the beauty of human art. Nothing in all creation lies outside its purview, for nothing in all creation is unrelated to the purposes of God.

In Scripture too we witness a conflict of world views not unlike that of today. Israel stood at variance with Babylonian, Egyptian and Canaanite beliefs and practices, not in minor details of tribal religion, but far more fundamentally in her overall understanding of God and his relationship to his creation. This creational theme pervades both Old and New Testaments. It shaped not only the prophets' response to their times (for example, Is 40—45), but also the apostle Paul's response to Greek modes of thought the early church encountered (for example, Acts 17:16-34 and Colossians). Theirs was a response that touched not only how people thought, but also how they acted in marriage and family, in their daily work and in their relationship to the government. A world view is involved at every level.

The history of Christian thought tells a similar story. Consider the range of concerns in the early church fathers and in St. Augustine's *City of God.* Consider the scope and systematic character of Aquinas's thinking, virtually unmatched today. Consider practitioners too—Christians in government, education, art and science—whose work was profoundly influenced by their faith. Relatively few of them systematically articulate a comprehensive world view, and in our day that has become too large a task for any one individual. One, like Calvin, might spell out an overall theological framework; another might speak to some particular area. But the Christian mind has been active and influential in the past, providing us with prototypes for the kind of responsible Christian thinking that is crucial today.

In considering a Christian world view, however, we must keep in mind that a Christian does not and cannot think in a closet, uninfluenced by other than biblical input alone. The Bible, after all, is not an exhaustive revelation about everything we might need to consider: there simply is not a decisive text for each issue we face today or in any other age. Yet we must learn to think biblically about the contributions of philosophy and psychology and art, and about values to pursue in the political and economic arenas. This means drawing on the overall framework of belief and of moral principles which the biblical writers brought to a multitude of different situations in different cultural and historical settings. It means building that framework and those principles into the Christian today.

Some of the early church fathers claimed that all truth is God's truth wherever it is found.[2] If something is true, then we can thank God for it. They recognized that the pagan mind had an incomplete picture of things and was in some things utterly wrong, but they also insisted that the Christian recapture those fragments of truth and restore them to the body of truth as a whole, to the right framework from which they were in effect torn. From a Christian perspective, all truth is about either God or God's creation or things God knows but never himself created—like technological and artistic possibilities he left for us to bring to actuality. Since it all relates to him in the end, we can embrace whatever things are true or just or lovely, for they declare the glory of God and show his handiwork.

The fact is that how we spell out a Christian view of things is influenced by many factors: Augustine and Aquinas made use of Greek ways of thinking, eighteenth-century Christians thought of the world in Newtonian terms, and today's Christian outlook reflects and responds to twentieth-century science and culture. The Greek mind saw everything in relation to eternally unchanging Forms, and Christians took those Forms to be the eternal wisdom of God exhibited in his creation. Their thinking about nature, art, ethics, jurisprudence and so forth, all followed from this. In other words, the overall conceptual model of the day to which Christians must relate their beliefs—and in the West it is generally a scientific model—provides a vehicle for fleshing out our understanding. We need to relate our faith to the behavioral and social sciences as they are today, as well as the natural sciences, if we are to articulate a world view that makes sense to the contemporary mind.

There is, in other words, a history of Christian activity in the world of thought, not all of it equally perceptive or developed to be sure, but Christians throughout the centuries have made their beliefs and values felt. So it must be now. In my own discipline, for example, a tradition of Christian philosophical activity can be traced from Augustine to our own day, a tradition in which Christian perspectives are put to constructive work.[3] Augustine converted the archetypal Forms in the eternal Mind of Neo-Platonic thought into the wisdom of the Creator-Logos, Jesus Christ. It was basically this which opened the door to a thousand years of Christian philosophical activity, that gave new shape to Western thought and new purpose to Western culture. In the context of seventeenth- and eighteenth-century mechanistic science, Descartes, Berkeley, Leibniz and others developed metaphysical schemes designed to exhibit the place of God and of human freedom in what seemed otherwise to be a completely material world. Their contributions continue to influence modern thought. In the nineteenth century, Søren Kierkegaard gave to the human person a passionate inwardness rarely articulated before, thereby bringing into focus a depth of faith unknown to the Enlightenment mind and a self-giving love quite alien to the romanticist. In all of this, Christian perspectives were at work. So they are in the analytic philosophy of today, as Christians address fundamental issues with a kind of competence that keeps Christianity in the marketplace of ideas.

The diversity in Christian thinking is inevitably such that no one formulation can be taken as final. Our knowledge is far too incomplete for that, and we are too history-bound. We know in part, and we see through a glass darkly. But a long tradition of such activity does exist, on which we build and from which we still learn, even while we try to assimilate new knowledge and new forms of thought and art and culture.

A Christian world view is pluralistic for a further reason, namely, that Christian theology itself embraces a number of different traditions. Reformed theology differs enough from Lutheran theology, and from Mennonite theology, and from Thomistic theology, that attitudes to philosophy and art and science tend to differ too. Christian attitudes also differ in regard to particular psychological or economic theories. We have a unifying framework of essential biblical faith, but it is construed somewhat differently in various Christian traditions as it interacts with the changing state of academic disciplines and cultural expression.

This kind of pluralism can be extremely beneficial. Its very presence offsets lopsided emphases, counters premature dogmatism, encourages self-criticism, aids the improvement of understanding and provides alternate avenues to explore. It reminds us of our finiteness, our creatureliness, our humanity; without that awareness a world view could not be Christian at all.

Nicholas Wolterstorff points out that in any discipline a theory is accountable both to what we take as data (our *data beliefs*) and to the larger body of theories we already hold (our *control beliefs*).[4] Among all of a person's control beliefs, religious beliefs and values (or else religion-substitutes) play a decisive part. But several different theories might be equally consonant with Christian control beliefs so that a Christian world view could take several different directions. Likewise one and the same theory might prove acceptable to both Christian and non-Christian control beliefs, so that areas of agreement between Christian and non-Christian world views appear.

The point is twofold: first, if not just one Christian view of everything is possible, then Christian thinking, for all its common framework, admits of pluralism. It is not a monolithic, closed system, but an ongoing exploratory task. Second, if the same view can sometimes be acceptable to both Christian and non-Christian, then in that regard a Christian may find common ground and make common cause with others. What distinguishes a Christian world view is not that every detail of its application and articulation is uniquely Christian, but rather that the overall framework is biblical, and the rest of its many manifestations in our lives fits naturally with that. But which particular formulation one prefers may depend on theological considerations (compare Mennonite and Reformed views of war, for example) or it may not.

At times in the past, this emphasis on control beliefs and religious presuppositions would have been criticized as allowing a lack of objectivity. Science was supposed to be presuppositionless, empirical observation value-free, and scholarship meant religious and moral neutrality. But the myth of complete objectivity has been exploded. The demand for value-free science itself makes a value judgment; it comes loaded with dubious presuppositions about both knowledge and human nature. Factual inquiry, we now see, is theory-laden, and work in the history of science has revealed how crucial sociological factors in a scientific community can be in resisting (or accepting) changes in acceptable theory. Rationalism's demand for purely objective arguments, like positivism's demand for purely objective confirmations, has become indefensible. But if other more subjective factors influence what people think, then world-viewish beliefs and values cannot be excluded. We all think from some perspective or another, consciously so or not. Intellectual honesty consists rather in identifying one's perspectives, in tracing their impact openly and in being willing to examine their credibility.[5]

An overall world view, then, will have the following characteristics:

1. It has a *wholistic* goal, trying to see every area of life and thought in an integrated fashion.

2. It is a *perspectival* approach, coming at things from a previously adopted point of view which now provides an integrative framework.

3. It is an *exploratory* process, probing the relationship of one area after another to the unifying perspective.

4. It is *pluralistic* in that the same basic perspective can be articulated in somewhat different ways.

5. It has *action outcomes*, for what we think and what we value guide what we will do.

God the Creator

What distinguishes a Christian world view from its competitors is the basic framework of biblical thought within which it operates and within which every aspect of the biblical drama is set. Stated simply, this framework is the ongoing relationship between God and his creation. Within this relationship God's providence is at work; so too are human sin and God's grace, Christ's Incarnation and his promised kingdom of justice and peace. The God-creation relationship then must be the overall biblical framework for Christian thinking and doing.

An initial caution is necessary. In speaking of the God-creation *relationship,* I have in mind far more than the fact that God originally brought things into being. That too easily runs into a sidetrack if we spend our energies debating how God did it and when, rather than asking why and following this main line of inquiry into the wide-ranging significance of creation.

Once we take the main line we immediately realize that the biblical picture of the God-creation relationship distinguishes a Christian world view from its competitors. Naturalistic world views, by contrast, have a monistic or one-level framework: God is out of the picture, and the entire creation becomes nothing more than an array of physical occurrences with unplanned side effects. Pantheistic world views blur the distinction between God and his creation, so that the active kind of relationship we find in the Bible is either forgotten, or else taken to symbolize the general presence of the divine in everything there is. Some liberal theologians have the same tendency. By making God an immanent presence in nature or the human spirit, thereby downplaying his transcendence, they not only reinterpret revelation and redemption as natural historical developments, but they also come closer to monism than to the two-level framework of the God-creation relationship. Among the different theistic religions, too, important differences arise: biblical Christianity gives a much fuller account of the God-creation relationship than do either Judaism or Islam. The Incarnation of Christ and his redemptive work dramatically reveal God's purpose and love to an extent that is unknown elsewhere. In this consummate action of the God-creation relationship, then, we have the watershed between Christian and non-Christian world views.

But what actual difference does it make? How does something as general as God's relationship to his creation affect art and science and the business world and our social problems? If we are to apply it in our thinking, we need a clearer picture of this overall framework. Consider then the following ingredients in the biblical picture.

1. *God creates freely.* Being self-sufficient, God was not compelled to create but did so freely. He did not have to create this particular world, but chose it out of many possible worlds he might have made. Nor is he compelled to act as he does now: he chooses to do so out of who he is and for his own purposes.

To believe in God, to trust his ways, is then to accept the way we, and all that is, are made. We will enter into his enjoyment of things, celebrating his works, not as a burden but because we are honored to do so, and we will do so freely and heartily. A positive attitude to life should result, and a healthy self-acceptance.

2. *All creation has value.* At the outset, God called each part of it "good" and, thinking of the whole, pronounced it "very good" (Gen 1:4, 10, 12, 18, 21, 25, 31). These were positive value judgments, and whatever moral evil we now find has come subsequently to mar the scene. That there are vast possibilities in his creation which God still finds of value is evident from his investment in it, revealing himself to us, incarnating himself in our world and suffering to save it. On this account nature is not divine, as some of the Greeks supposed; nor is it intrinsically evil, to be shunned in otherworldly ways, as some Christians as well as Eastern mystics have thought. Rather it is God's handiwork, the theater in which his play is running, in which we are both actors and audience at the same time. If God so values his creation and gives himself to it, then we should too for his sake, prizing the good possibilities it holds for human learning and culture and well-being.

3. *Creation is ordered,* law-governed in ways that reflect the wisdom and purposes of God. Its regularities make life, as well as human understanding and art, at all possible. Science depends on repeatable experiments; it formulates hypotheses and makes predictions; it develops a body of theory, and on that basis technology is advanced.

But all of this assumes some kind of uniformity in nature, an intelligible order that we can trace.

Art too requires an ordered world. The painter depends on pigments that will work; the musician counts on an ordered scale. The aesthetic uses of sight and sound, texture and rhythm, that so delight our senses, are only possible in an ordered world.

Human behavior too is, in measure, predictable, for we live in a common world with common needs, sharing a generically alike human nature that we can in good measure understand. An ordered society, moreover, is possible because we are part of an ordered world. Seeing the world as God's creation stirs interest in the kinds of just social order that might be developed, in comparison to the all-too-prevalent inequities and antagonisms we find in the world today. An ordered creation leads to optimism about social change, as well as about increases of knowledge and the flowering of art.

4. *God has delegated powers to what he made,* so that nature's processes function of themselves without constant chaos on the one hand, or constant miraculous intervention on the other. This is our Father's world. It follows that we can do things with what science teaches of the world around us, and with what human psychology and social studies teaches us also.

As human persons we possess divinely delegated powers, astoundingly somewhat Godlike abilities and matching responsibilities as well. We remain creatures, of course, dependent on God both for being and for being what we are. We are governed by his laws. Yet he has mandated us to be his responsible agents too. There is a creation mandate, creational tasks to be done, in work that harnesses global resources to meet human needs and provide an appropriate quality of life that honors the Creator. In a world with such resources, people possessing God-given abilities should not always expect miracles, any more than Jesus himself did in his temptation here on earth. Rather we look to what God has already provided, concentrating on the development and stewardship of economic, medical, intellectual, aesthetic and people resources that are available already. Human creativity, finite though it is, still images God's. Creative thinking, creative technology, creative management, creative art, creative people—these are good gifts we should be developing and directing for just and loving ends in this world. God has entrusted his creatures with these powers.

5. *God remains creatively involved.* He is by nature creative and did not stop being so on the seventh day. He remains the living Lord, active in history and in the lives of his people. The Old Testament record is filled with his involvement, his providence and his direction. What could be more creative than the coming of Christ to make things new? What is more creative than a "new creation"?

This always-creative God is called Emmanuel, "God with us," for his creative activity is present with ours in every area a biblical world view touches. Here is the basis for hope, the confident expectation that God's purposes for his creation will in the end be fulfilled. Here too is meaning to life's efforts, assured by the knowledge that God is still working with us in this world.

6. *God's purposes are evident in the way he has ordered his creation,* and the laws that govern things are intended to actualize what God purposed and what he values most. Here is the basis for various kinds of *natural law* ethics, which throughout the centuries have been a major Christian approach to moral matters. Why, for example, do the Ten Commandments forbid adultery? The answer is found by appealing to the inherent nature of the human sexual relationship: its biological potential for reproduction and its psychological potential for renewing again and again the mutual devotion that bonds a couple together. These point to God's purposes for sex and to the marriage relationship. Similar considerations give rise to Christian concern over abortion on demand: respect for God's purposes, in making the reproductive process as he did, requires respect for even the early fetus that has a natural potential for full personhood. This religious attitude to life is likely to differ sharply from a purely naturalistic world view, where there is no Creator-God whose purposes we regard.

This kind of creational ethic speaks to the purposes of work and play. It gave rise to the Western belief in equal human rights, for in creating us all human, God intended that we be treated equally as humans, with the right to what being human requires. John

Locke therefore insisted that God gave us rights to life, to liberty and to the property needed to sustain a human quality of life. These are not unconditional, unlimited rights, but are limited by other people's rights. Under certain conditions, as in criminal punishment, a particular right may even be abrogated. America's founding fathers included the pursuit of happiness in our basic rights, not in the hedonistic sense of selfishly maximizing pleasure, but with reference to the satisfaction that comes from exercising our God-given capacities. Freedom is not an individual's right to do whatever quirky things he pleases, regardless of others, but the liberty to exercise essential human rights while respecting similar rights in others. All persons equally must be respected.

In regard to ethics, therefore, the God-creation relation under-scores the value of what God intended for his creation; it alerts us to moral indicators, like natural laws, in the way things are made; it presents us with a mandate, an obligation in fact, to respect human rights. And this has social and political consequences.[6]

Being Human in God's Creation

Within God's creation, the distinctive nature and value of human beings stands out, and the consequences of thinking about people in this context are vast. The dominant popular conception, how-ever, is very individualistic. Each of us is, as it were, an island, try-ing to find herself, discovering other people, struggling for individ-ual fulfillment, asking what life is all about and whether God is real. Some approaches to psychological counseling take this sort of thing to be normative, even pander to it, as if the meaning-giving center of a person's life is within herself. By taking such a view, we have reduced social institutions to human inventions, products of history at best based on common consent and at worst arbitrary and irrelevant encrustations. Marriage is either an unnecessary bond or else a purely contractual arrangement; governmental authority rests on a tacit social contract; and even religion becomes a private matter, an affair of the individual heart. We have even democra-tized our relationship to God and made it appear quite optional.

This individualistic view of people and society developed in the seventeenth and eighteenth centuries, partly under the influence of the atomistic view of nature in the science of the day, partly out of Renaissance emphases on human values and human freedom, and partly as an alternative to the highly authoritarian structures of medieval church and feudal society. It drew on the belief in God-given human rights that developed during the late Middle Ages, but it has now come to the point that liberty seems tantamount to license.

Emphasizing the individual originally provided a needed counter-balance and brought many beneficent consequences. But individu-*alism* takes selfish extremes, virtually deifying the individual and absolutizing freedom. Philosophically, the results can be seen in Nietzsche's "will to power" or Sartre's "dreadful freedom"; psychologically, in narcissism and the almost cultic quest for individual fulfillment; sociologically, in the erosion of the family; politically, in conducting government by "balance of interests" and "balance of power." We live for our own individual ends and social groups, forgetting how essential relationships are to human nature in general, as well as to one's own identity as "me."

1. *In biblical perspective we are not isolated individuals, but relational beings through and through.* The most pervasive theme, after all, is that we live within the relationship of God to his creation—we exist in relation to God. We are not self-made, but draw from him our very existence, every good thing we are and have, our purpose, our meaning, our hope. In him we live and work and have our being, and to him we are ever accountable. As Augustine said, "Thou hast made us for thyself, O God, and our hearts are restless until they rest in thee." In Reinhold Niebuhr's words, our center, the real focus of our lives, is *outside* ourselves, not within. We bear God's image, ineradicably so, and whether we admit it or not we are in our heart of hearts religious beings. Out of this heart, our relationship to God, flow all the issues of life. Everything takes its place in that context. This is the watershed between theistic and nontheistic views of the human person.

2. *I cannot live this relationship to God as an isolated individual, alone.* I am a created part of nature and society, created a relational being, to

live in constant *relation to the physical world* and to other people.

In regard to the physical, our genetic identity is there, our nourishment, the work of our hands, our senses and emotions, our arts and crafts, science and technology, even our eternal destiny in the resurrection of the body. Jesus himself was born of woman, worked as a carpenter, hungered and thirsted, suffered and died, and rose physically from the dead.

The Christian mind, then, can never belittle the physical or our involvements in it. Behavioral studies that stress psychological and environmental conditioning are at once legitimized. The physical and economic conditions in which people live become an intense concern.

On the other hand, the Greek dichotomy of body and soul has at times been adopted as Christian, encouraging an otherworldly mystical path and an ascetic approach to life that takes physical pleasure to be evil. That kind of extreme is missing from the more wholistic biblical account. Socrates saw his own execution as freeing his mind from bodily distractions. But for the Christian, any belittling of death because of the life to come is, as it were, a slap at the Creator for making us the physical beings we are. Death remains an enemy. When Lazarus died, Jesus wept.

As a creature of God I live my relationship to God in relation to nature, responsible to "handle with care" the physical, the economic, the psychological and of course the environment with its natural resources and aesthetic possibilities.

3. *We are created in relation to one another.* Old Testament people had their identity in family, tribe and nation, a corporate identity rather than the individualistic "me." Who am I? I have a family name, a wife and children, friends. I teach people, I belong to a particular church, I am a citizen of this country. *That* is who I am: not so much *in*dependent as *inter*dependent through and through, and I am responsible to God in all these regards.

I do not face these responsibilities alone, for certain social institutions are divinely ordained for our benefit. Marriage is not just a contractual arrangement, though its legalization is important. Government is not just a contractual arrangement either, though having a constitution is important. Economic activity, work, too is ordained by God and so of course is the church. The particular organizational form these institutions follow changes historically, but their underlying purposes are unchanging, rooted in what it ideally is to be a human person in God's creation. A Christian world view, then, will talk of God's purpose for marriage, for government, for the economic sphere and for work, as well as for the church. It will scrutinize the forms that social institutions take, as means to pursuing God's purposes with justice and with love. The kingdom ideal of *shalōm* must stand before us whenever we think of the human society. Shalom means peace, yes, but the peace that flows from equal justice and economic sufficiency, a justice that frees from fear and want, and fills the heart with joyful praise.

4. *To act responsibly in these many regards requires understanding and right values.* So *aims for education* come into focus too. The arts and sciences will help us understand the range of life's concerns, moral education will help establish values, biblical and theological input can ground the Christian mind, while philosophy wrestles with the basic assumptions on which all of these depend. The overall framework of a Christian world view begins to be filled out.

But Christian thinking is a process that never finishes in this life, and fresh value judgments must again and again be made. So education must develop the capacity to think and make judgments aright: research skills, analytic and critical skills (recognizing assumptions, formulating and evaluating arguments, accumulating experience, gaining wisdom). Education must develop the ability to communicate if people are to act responsibly in this world: interpersonal dynamics, verbal skills, artistic and persuasive uses of language, and on it can go. Education should prepare us for responsible action, not only in job plus church, but also in family life and social life and citizenship and in continued intellectual and aesthetic growth—for all these are divinely created channels in which we live our relationship to God, to nature and to others.

5. *The presence of sin and grace must be recognized.* Here too a Christian view stands in contrast to much that circulates today. We tend to think of sin atomistically: much as we suppose society to be made

up of isolated individuals, so too we suppose that sin consists of isolated, independent mistakes. The only real relationship of one mistake to another is that of a bad example. This was the Pelagian view which the church rejected in the fifth century and which was more a part of the Greek world view than of a biblical one. Pelagius accepted the ancient idea that we are ruled by reason, so that all we need in order to do what is right is to know what is right, whether by instruction or example. Sin is due to ignorance, a particular sin due to some particular ignorance. Consistent with this, Pelagius saw God's saving grace as the provision of good examples, especially the supreme example of Jesus.

But he kept the subject out of its proper framework. The most basic and essential thing about people is not that we are rational beings, however much influenced by reason's instruction and examples, but that we exist in relation to our Creator. Sin is rooted in what happens to that God-creation relationship, for what happens there has a pervasive influence on everything else about us and every kind of thing we think and do.

The apostle Paul saw this clearly when he traced individual sins to a refusal to have God in our knowledge, so that we "worship and serve the creature" rather than the Creator (Rom 1). This elevation of the creature to the place of God is a denial of our own creature-liness. It strikes at the very heart of what it is to be human. Out of this root issues life's variety of particular sins.

Augustine saw this clearly too, and he was Pelagius's principal critic. In the final analysis, he argued, we are not ruled by what we know but by what we most love, for we are not just rational but relational beings after all. As God's creatures, made for him and not just for ourselves, loved by him and not just by ourselves, our hearts are restless until they rest in him. The moral law, indeed the natural law, is therefore summed up in what Jesus called the first commandment, that we should love the Lord God with all our being. Sin, said Augustine, is unnaturally disordered love. When this natural order is disrupted, then other loves are affected too, other relationships suffer. Sin is thus not a matter of individual errors; it is a pervasive human condition at the heart of our lives.

Human relationships get twisted out of shape. We have broken marriages, prodigal children, sexual abuse, international conflicts. Government serves special interests, rather than equal justice for all. Business motivated by greed manipulates the public, profligately creating worthless appetites rather than serving real human needs. Social evils abound; people suffer. In the final analysis the cause is to be found in our relationship to God.

Of particular concern is the idea that environment is to blame. The romanticist notion is an obvious example: left to themselves without the repressive artificiality of social institutions, people and their relationships would all be benign and flourish. The Marxist echoes this idea when he traces the ultimate cause to the socioeconomic struggle; others might point to repressed desires or to early maladjustments; others again point out that individually and collectively we are still immature, still in need of growth. All these play their parts, to be sure, but the root of sin lies deeper than any of these and is certainly more than the fact that we are immature.

Again the overall framework of thought is fundamentally awry. It does not look beyond people in relationship, people in a physical environment, people in an institutionalized society. It fails to see all this within the still larger horizon of a creation in relationship to God. But if the latter is true, then personal maturity and social adjustment, social reform and even revolution must be kept in larger perspective and not become the focus of all our hopes. The need for social change is undeniable. The Old Testament prophets would criticize the political and economic structures of our day, as they did theirs. But in the final analysis saving grace that reconciles us to the Creator brings hope and healing to all the alienated of earth. The kingdom of shalom must come.

A Final Frame of Reference
A Christian world view then will culminate in a Christian view of history as an arena for God's continued creativity. Nature's processes and the social institutions he has ordained, especially that body of believers which is his church, all these serve God's purposes on earth. All contribute in his kingdom. And so does the history of

ideas, so do the minds of men and women. But history is more than a random collection of parts. If the heavens declare the glory of God, so too does history tell of his handiwork, and so too does the Christian mind.

The kingdom still awaits its king. Yet even our perception of this hope, and of the God-creation framework for life and thought, is limited by our finite understanding and twisted by our sinful bent. We too easily misunderstand. Our response comes slowly, partially, faultily, as well. It is not easy to see and do what is implied by the fact that God creates freely, that all creation has value and is ordered and empowered for his good purposes, and that God is still creatively involved. Nor is it easy to think and live our relation to God in this overall context, in relation to nature and other persons. Such is the human condition.

Yet in God's kingdom, salvation applies to all existence, the human mind included. To capture the modern mind for Christ is therefore essential. Malik is right. And to develop and implement a Christian world view for our times in the major areas of learning and life is what that mandate entails.[7]

2
Christian World Views and Some Lessons of History

Mark A. Noll

Comprehensive and coherent Christian thinking has never been a major part of religious life in America. The emphasis in this country has rested much more with activity, energetic attention to problem solving and a preference for the accomplishments of know-how. In many ways these characteristics have produced good results for Christians. Americans have been activists in missions and reform movements, and we have been energetic in founding a Christian agency or two for almost every conceivable human need. In still other ways affecting intellectual life, however, the results have been less favorable.[1]

Problems for Christian thinking from our activism are now compounded by the experience-oriented nature of our age. We are everywhere urged to grab all the gusto (since we only go around once), to get in touch with our feelings and to realize our self-potential in the immediate present. There are many problems here. One of the most serious is that when Christians accept such appeals without serious qualification, they forfeit a heritage which has prized thought as well as feeling, reflection as well as experience.

To be sure, hard intellectual labor has not always led to a healthy church. Sometimes, in fact, the pursuit of learning has been a means to escape the claims of the gospel or the requirements of God's law. It is also true that vital Christianity has existed, at least for brief periods, without a noticeable increase in seriousness about the intellect. Yet generally, where Christian faith is securely rooted, where it penetrates deeply into a culture to change the lives of individuals and of larger groups, where it continues for more than a generation as a living testimony to the grace of God—in such situations, we almost invariably find Christians ardently cultivating the intellect for the glory of God.

The construction of Christian world views has been an ongoing task throughout the history of the church. From that history it is possible to draw at least three generalizations:

1. The importance of Christian world views is evident from the beginnings of Christianity itself.

2. Dynamic Christian movements which have exerted a long-lasting influence have always involved the evangelization of the mind.

3. Failure to work at taking the mind captive for Christ invariably leads to the weakening or the collapse of Christian vitality.

These three generalizations are amply illustrated in the lengthy annals of "ancient history" and in the story of America as well. But before turning to consider these general lessons and their specific relevance to Americans, it is worth lingering over the two phrases "Christian world views" and "Christian thinking." For historical purposes the second of these is more helpful than the first. What we find when we examine the past is that Christians have been working in many different ways to devote their thinking to Christ. Believers in past times have not so much *had* world views as they have been struggling between competing conceptions of the world. Or they have been pushing out from narrow, parochial thinking toward broader considerations. Or they have been wrestling to understand Scripture with the thought patterns of their own time while trying to mold those thought patterns according to the guidelines of the Bible. In all of this what turns out to be most exemplary is not so much the result as the process. This does not mean that the results of these efforts are insignificant. It means rather that wholehearted pursuit of the ideal of being "transformed by the renewal of your mind" (Rom 12:2) can strengthen the church even when later Christians disagree with some results of an earlier process. Christian world views are always in the process of reformation. The most encouraging lesson of history is how many believers have worked at that process and how life changing have been the results.

World Views and the Foundation

From one angle, the entire history of salvation can be regarded as an ongoing series of relationships. God chose to make the world and humans to live in it. God chose to show himself to Noah, Abraham, Moses and to the people of Israel under the kings. God gave himself most lovingly and most definitively to his creatures in the person of Christ. God established his people through the apostles as a communion to draw members of every tribe and nation to himself. God promises to bring history to a climactic conclusion by establishing the reign of Christ forever. From this perspective, the work of God looks like only a series of actions for which hard and careful thinking is mostly irrelevant.

Nothing, however, could be further from the truth. The activity of God in human history has been laden with conceptual meanings at every step along the way. It has been an activity for which God himself provided authoritative explanation, commentary and exposition in the pages of Scripture. And that activity, no less than its record in the Bible, has always involved cohesive conceptions of the world at large. Put another way, Christian world views are part and parcel of the gospel message from its earliest beginnings.

As other chapters of this book make clear, even the earliest words in the Bible reflect the importance of world views. The book of Genesis reveals God as the fountain of creation and his glory as the end of life. Neither nature by itself nor people are divine, as the world views of the Babylonians and Egyptians held. The biblical account of creation tells a story, but a story which carries with it a comprehensive attitude toward the world.

The same is true for the rest of the Old Testament. The great

lawgiver Moses, the prophets, and the writers of Psalms and Prov-
erbs operated from within a singular conception of the world. The
word of God to the Hebrews and his actions among them bore conceptual freight. Thus, the prophets spoke of the peace and security
which God brings as *shalōm*, a concept which means not only cessa-
tion of toil, not only an end of strife, but also a positive conception
of righteousness which imitates God's own moral purity. Prophets
and psalmists spoke of humans as living *souls (nepesh)*, but they did
not mean, as in the Greek thought of Socrates, a disembodied Form
chained piteously to the materiality of the world. Rather they
meant by a *soul* a creature uniquely imaging God's own vitality. A
soul was not a divisible amalgam of body, will and spirit, but a unity
that lived amid creation, acted with moral responsibility and found
true contentment only in service to God. We do not grasp the
richness of the Old Testament's announcement of God's power and
mercy, the depths of its meaning for human existence, until we
perceive the world view through which God chose to reveal
himself.[2]

Much the same may be said of the New Testament. Here a
dimension of Hellenistic, or later Greek thought, is added to the
solid Hebrew, or Semitic, basis of the Old Testament. The apostle
John picks up the Hellenistic term *logos* to apply to Jesus in the first
chapter of his Gospel. And here we have a most sensitive blending
of world views. The Greek sense of logos (*rationality* or *speech*) takes
on an embodied Semitic character when John tells us that the logos
became flesh and dwelt among us; and that through this logos we
behold God's glory. Without a realization of the world views within
which a concept like logos had meaning, it would be as if John began
his Gospel with an irrelevant digression. But to realize how John
put such a term to use is to realize the uniquely three-dimensional
character of God's revelation of himself.

In the first centuries A.D. the church faced the need to define the
nature of Christ's own person and especially his relationship to God
the Creator. For this purpose, Christians struggled through many
difficulties as they applied Hellenistic thought to the basically
Semitic revelation of Scripture. The struggle was a long one, from

the midthird to the midfifth century precisely because every one of the terms at issue was part of complex world views. Was Jesus two *persons* (God and man) or one *person* with two *substances?* Was Jesus *like* God the Father or *the same as* the Father? For each of these questions, and many more besides, several answers were proposed, and often several answers within both the Latin- and Greek-speaking parts of the church.

The church's final decisions on these matters came only after agonizing controversy. Jesus was "of one substance with the Father" (Creed of Nicea, 325); he was "one and the same Christ, Son, Lord, only-begotten, made known in two natures without confusion, without change, without division, without separation" (Definition of Chalcedon, 451). These decisions do not answer every last question concerning Jesus' divine and human character, but they have served the church very well over the centuries. And one of the primary reasons why they have served the church so well is that they were hammered out so self-consciously with regard to prevailing world views.[3]

In the earliest consciousness of Christians, God's loving actions to Israel and then in Christ remained the focus for worship and life. But what these actions *meant*, for the immediate recipients as well as for Christians who came later, depended at every stage on the nature of the world views in which they were interpreted.

Evangelizing the Mind

During the subsequent unfolding of history, Christian movements of long-lasting significance regularly involved thinking at the most serious levels. Only rarely did such movements begin as intellectual efforts as such. Much more often they came into existence out of deep inner responses to God's grace. Yet as such movements developed, they showed great concern as well for shaping the way in which Christians viewed the world at large.

Two of the best examples of this process are the monastic movements of the Middle Ages and the Protestant Reformation. Both began with godly reformers sensing the need for a more genuine spirituality. Both went on to create institutions and to engage in practical Christian service. Both passed through periods of stagnation and renewal. And in spite of inevitable limitations, both showed how important it was to capture the mind for Christ.

The Monastic Movement. It is only a slight exaggeration to say that the influence of monks lay behind everything of Christian value during the Middle Ages, the years from roughly A.D. 350 to 1400. To be sure, the monastic movement had high points and low points. Its great moments included the days of the earliest monks in Egypt during the fourth and fifth centuries. These pioneers perceived correctly that the church's success in the world had left its inner spiritual life in jeopardy. When the church became the only official religion of the Roman Empire during the fourth century, its attention turned increasingly to self-serving exercises of power. In reaction, the monks went out singly into the desert or hid themselves away in small groups in order to recover the God of moral purity and supernatural grace for whom the "Christian world" had little time.

Another great moment came when Benedict of Nursia (ca 480-ca 550), distressed by the immorality in the church and society of Rome, founded monastic communities, including a central house at Monte Cassino, in the early sixth century. Benedict's "Rule," a set of regulations which became the model for other monastic communities, included the significant injunction that "the brothers ought to be occupied in manual labour; and . . . in sacred reading."[4] Then after a period of decline came the founding in 910 of the great monastery at Cluny in France from which emerged the inspiration, and many of the leaders, for renewal over the next three hundred years of the church's history. Finally the Dominicans and Franciscans appeared during the thirteenth century. These were new orders for monks among the people, or friars, who took the entire known world as their parish.

These great pulses of monastic reform all had certain things in common. They all encouraged serious contemplation of God. They all acknowledged the desperateness of the human condition apart from God. They all turned people inward to meditate on Scripture and to ponder the mercies of Christ. They all encouraged heroic missionary efforts and practical aid for the downtrodden. And they all promoted serious learning as an offering to the Lord.

The intellectual activity of the monks during the so-called Dark Ages is well known. When the light of learning flickered low in Europe, monks preserved the precious texts of Scripture and other Christian writings. Monks kept alive an interest in the languages. Monks founded schools which eventually became the great universities of Europe. Monks, in short, preserved the life of the mind when almost no one else was giving it a thought. And in so doing, by God's grace, they preserved the church.

Thomas Aquinas. The culmination of intellectual activity among the monks was the work of Thomas Aquinas (ca 1225-1274). Aquinas was a Dominican friar who composed hymns, wrote biblical commentaries, preached, prepared manuals for missionary work among the Muslims, spent long hours in contemplating the work of Christ and almost single-handedly reconstructed systematic Christian thinking. His most notable achievement was to enlist the teaching of Aristotle, newly rediscovered in Europe, for Christianity. He took Aristotle's conception that reality was an essential interweaving of Form and matter to make Christian arguments for the existence of God and the plausibility of the Incarnation. And he took Aristotle's analysis of action, broken down into four different kinds of *causes*, to explore the meaning of the creation in human terms. In all this, Thomas devoted rigorous intellectual efforts, as G. K. Chesterton once put it, to "the praise of Life, the praise of Being, the praise of God as the Creator of the World."[5]

Aquinas's work left important legacies. He provided an example for examining together both the world we experience through the senses and the truths we read in Scripture. He provided a theoretical basis for some of the "mysteries" of the church like the Lord's Supper. And he proposed a model for apologetics which respected the intellect of non-Christians as well as the missionary mandate for believers. In an age where the thought forms of Aristotle had come to dominate learned discourse, he taught Aristotle to "speak like a Christian" and so preserved the conceptual power of Christian faith and its ability to speak to his time.

Thomas did not provide the last word on any of these matters. Martin Luther and John Calvin, for example, felt that Aquinas had overemphasized what we learn about God from nature at the expense of what we learn from Scripture. Yet what Thomas did provide was a formulation of the faith which encouraged his contemporaries to labor with their minds for the glory of God. And in doing this, he left an intellectual perspective and a body of writing which have helped sustain the wider Christian church to this very day.

The Reformation. During the early period of the Reformation in the sixteenth century, formal learning seemed almost irrelevant to the spiritual activity of the day. Connections between the Catholic Church and Europe's educational institutions seemed to make the entire life of the mind suspect. The Protestant commitment to the priesthood of believers and to the activity of the Holy Spirit in the entire church seemed to put in doubt the need for special efforts in learning. Was not merely "the Bible alone" and the inner testimony of the Holy Spirit sufficient for all that was necessary in life?

The counterargument—that mental activity was essential for Christian life—came from the leading Protestants themselves.[6] They saw quickly that the cultivation of a reformed spirituality required attention to world views. Martin Luther (1483-1546) argued forcefully that if people were to understand such truths as "justification by faith," they must know both the world of Scripture and the needs of their own day. In often brutally frank language he chastised parents for neglecting the education of their children, precisely because all children needed to be instructed in what the contemporary world, the Scriptures and the traditions of history, actually *meant*. Without such attention to consistent and coherent thinking, the Reformation would spin off into countless individualistic whims, marked not by godliness but by idiosyncracies. Furthermore, insistence on the "priesthood of believers" demanded that education be brought to the most ordinary levels and to the most ordinary people. Protestantism marks the start of universal education in Europe because its leaders insisted that all individuals had the responsibility to understand the world in which they lived and the spiritual world held out to them by Christian teaching.

As a consequence of this defense of education, Protestants were active in establishing schools of all sorts. Some were merely replacements for the Catholic schools which had been abandoned in the early days of the Reformation. Others, however, were more innovative, with teaching directed in special ways to the very young, to girls and women (who had been largely excluded from formal education in the ancient world and the Middle Ages), and for vocational as well as academic purposes. Inevitably, where Protestant schools were strongest, the Protestant Reformation made its greatest impact.

John Calvin. Perhaps the most significant of the Protestant efforts to construct a distinctly Christian world view took place in the Geneva of John Calvin (1509-1564). From his earliest days in that city, Calvin worked to instruct the mind and inspire the heart together. Calvin's theology was not intellectualist; he believed that the Spirit was necessary to change the heart before the mind would accept the gospel. And he felt that God manifested his sovereignty over every part of life. Yet Calvin also believed that the Spirit of God had created the world so that it could be observed. He believed that the Spirit had enabled nonbelievers correctly to understand nature and the human relationships of life. These activities of the Spirit, therefore, deserved consistent attention in order to shape the minds of Christians to see all of life as the arena of God's activity. Calvin championed instruction in the home, through catechisms and other simple teaching devices. He broadened the scope of education for the young people of Geneva. And he founded an academy, or university, for more advanced study, to which Protestants came from all over Europe. There they found great seriousness about the Christian message itself, but also great seriousness about studying the classical languages, medicine, theories concerning the natural world and what we would today call politics and sociology.[7]

Calvin's synthesis, combining a high view of God's sovereignty with an earnestness about education, also characterized other parts of Protestant Europe, especially southern Germany, Holland, Scotland and certain parts of England. In these places the faith of the Reformation became as influential for the shaping of world views as Thomas Aquinas's work continued to be for many parts of Catholic Europe. The goal was to bring every aspect of life under the general guidance of Christian thinking, to have each question in life answered by an answer coming from a Christian perspective.

As a consequence, individuals in this Protestant Reformed tradition labored as scientists to do their scientific work to the praise of God. In so doing, they expressed their belief that God had made the natural world to be explored and that the results of such exploration showed forth his glory. Statesmen in this tradition worked to make political and social organizations reflect the norms of justice that they found in Scripture. In so doing, they examined the contrasting rights of individuals, kings and parliaments, and contributed to theories about democracy and the existence of republics. They did what they could to make life in society reflect the goodness of God.

The Legacy of the Middle Ages and the Reformation. The influence of these efforts is with us to this day. Historians and social scientists debate vigorously whether Max Weber was correct in perceiving a causal link between Protestant Calvinism and the rise of Western capitalism. But all commentators are agreed that these Protestants looked on economic life as a sphere of existence which belonged in a Christian view of the world. Historians of science debate the precise debt which Newton, Boyle, Harvey and other pioneers of the scientific revolution owed to this same theological orientation. But again they usually agree that some impetus for the efforts to master the physical world came from the Protestant desire to include nature within their world views.

Once again, as in the case with Aquinas, it is possible to ask whether the results of the Protestant activity have always been good ones. As an example, modern ecologists sometimes accuse Reformed Protestants of exploiting nature by abusing the theological concept of "stewardship." But whatever our conclusions concerning such specific issues, the larger aims of the Protestants still deserve attention. These aims were to take the sovereignty of God seriously for all of life. This meant that explicitly Christian values provided the foundation for ways of looking at the world. And it meant that the world views which resulted provided a platform from which to live out the gospel in the realities of day-to-day life. As a result of these efforts to think like Christians, Europe and the world were permanently changed. And since the sixteenth century the thinking of these early Protestants has remained a source of recurring inspiration for others who also desire to love God with all their minds.

Medieval monasticism and the Protestant Reformation have been among the most influential movements in the history of the church. Most Christians today are able to affirm the general goals of each movement. The monks preserved a genuine Christian element within a church compromised by its accommodation to the world. The early Protestants aspired to see a theology of divine sovereignty become a reality for theory and practice. Legitimate Christian criticisms of both movements remain. Yet the positive lessons they teach are more important. These lessons concern Christian faithfulness, immersion in Scripture, zeal to spread the gospel and commitment to wholistic Christian service. But they involved perhaps must of all the Christianization of thinking, the elaboration of Christian world views. And because this is so, Benedict and Thomas Aquinas, Luther and Calvin, though they are long dead, still speak clearly to believers today who pray for the renewal of the mind in Christ.

The Peril of Neglecting the Mind
If the history of Christianity shows how fruitful it can be to cultivate the mind for Christ, it also indicates how dangerous it can be to neglect such activity. A word of caution is in order at this point. Following *either* the intellectuals who criticize the life of simple piety *or* the advocates of Christian experience who attack the life of the mind may lead to difficulty. The gospel properly calls to the whole person. Nothing less will do. In keeping with the Bible's teaching concerning the various tasks given to different parts of the

body, we may naturally expect Christians in different times and places to stress some things rather than others. The danger arises when the parts of the body, which are to complement each other, go on the attack.

Church history contains a number of sobering examples of what happens when "spirituality" allows no time for self-conscious attention to world views. The path to danger is not always the same, but the results usually are: Christian faith degenerates, lapses into gross error, or simply passes out of existence.

The Albigenses. One of the more interesting protest movements of the Middle Ages, the Albigenses, illustrates how easy it is for Christian groups which undervalue the mind to lapse into the employment of non-Christian world views. The Albigenses are named for the region in southern France where they flourished in the twelfth and thirteenth centuries. They were a variation of the Cathari, or "Pure Ones," who in the Middle Ages attempted to keep themselves unspotted from the pollutions of the flesh.[8]

Beyond a doubt, the Albigenses possessed several exemplary traits. In contrast to many officials in the medieval Catholic Church, leaders of the Albigenses were moral and conscientious pastors. Albigenses in general knew the value of following God's law. Their ascetic conduct often shamed less scrupulous church members, and so they remained an object of respect among the common people of southern France for nearly two hundred years. In the thirteenth century, crusades and an inquisition destroyed the movement.

What is significant for our purposes is that the Albigenses made it a principle to slight formal intellectual work. They were moralists above all else. The only thing, it seemed, which mattered was to live without moral fault. This, from the perspective of the late twentieth century, may seem a worthy goal, until we see how thoroughly the Albigensian commitment to morality excluded cultivation of the mind. There was no interest in formal thought, even if there had been time. This was wasted effort which absorbed attention which was needed for cultivating the ascetic life.

This abandonment of the mind, however, encouraged a slide toward the ancient heresy of Manichaeism. This deviant belief, which had existed in various forms since the classical period, was dualistic; it made the sharpest distinction between the life of the spirit and the life of the body. To the Albigenses matter itself was evil. Redemption meant the freeing of the spirit from the body. With these beliefs the Albigenses were forced to interpret Scripture allegorically: Old Testament prophets could not have meant it literally when they urged the faithful to establish justice in Israel; Christ could never have taken on an actual body of flesh; the kingdom of God was an utterly ethereal thing, not something which begins in the day-to-day life of each believer during this age. Given the precommitments of the Manichaean world view, Albigenses found it necessary to twist the straightforward and intended meanings of the Bible. They had no time for the spirituality which Jesus brought. For the words and concepts of the Bible, they retained a great affection. But because they had adopted a world view opposed to that of the prophets, apostles and Jesus himself, they were forced to reinterpret biblical words and ideas in order to bring them into harmony with their underlying world view. The result was a group which did teach the church some valuable lessons about ethical seriousness. But it was also a group which, because it rejected the cultivation of thinking in principle, found itself trapped by a world view alien to the gospel.

Pietism. Another illustration of the perils involved in not treating the mind as a Christian resource involves aspects of the Pietist movements of the seventeenth and eighteenth centuries. In general, Pietism breathed a badly needed vitality into several varieties of Christian faith, whether Protestant Pietists in Germany, Holland, England and America; or their Catholic counterparts in France or other parts of southern Europe.[9]

The thrust of Pietism was to draw believers back from formal, dogmatic rigidity toward living Christian experience. This was a timely appeal, for much calcification had taken place in the years since the Reformation and Counter Reformation. And many valuable things came from Pietism. Pietists inaugurated the first widespread missionary movements among Protestants, they encouraged renewed seriousness about the priesthood of believers, they turned laypeople back to eager study of the Bible and they encouraged many acts of social compassion.

The intellectual problem was not so much one of Pietism in itself as with the excesses of Pietism. Pietists had rediscovered the truth that Christianity is a life as well as a set of beliefs. The difficulty came when some Pietists began to view Christian faith as only a life, without a concern for beliefs at all. This led to fascination with practice, deep involvement in spiritual experience and absorption in the psychological dimensions of the faith. Objective realities of revelation were sometimes almost totally eclipsed. In the early nineteenth century, certain Christian teachers trained by Pietists even began to argue that "a feeling of dependence" was the foundation of Christianity. Others hesitated to affirm that God could break into the world in ways unknown to human experience.[10] These proposals proved destructive to the Christian faith which had been handed down since the time of the apostles. Always the church had had a place for Christian experience, but in living communion with the objective character of the gospel. Pietists quite properly protested when this objectivity came to be regarded as the sum and substance of the faith. But a few overreacted by picturing the *experience* of faith as the new totality.

At its extreme, the Pietist emphasis on religious life tended to subordinate self-conscious efforts to form Christian perspectives on the world. To be consumed by feeling was to have no time for thinking through the relationship between God and his creation. Once this place had been reached, it soon became difficult to distinguish between those forms of feeling which remained within the Christian orbit and those which had spun off as meteorites with no fixed center. Pietism played an important role in the revitalization of the church in the seventeenth and eighteenth centuries. Unchecked Pietism, however, also played a role in the coming of theological liberalism, nature mysticism and the humanistic romanticism of the nineteenth and twentieth centuries as well.

Albigenses and extreme Pietists teach modern believers a complex lesson. Both groups contributed something important to the Christian church. Both drew attention to matters needing reform. The problem in both cases, however, arose when a necessary means of renewal became the sum of the faith, when a part of the more general Christian life arose to dominate the whole. An attack on self-conscious Christian thinking was the cause of special difficulty. It meant the actual disappearance of the faith, its captivity by alien philosophies, or its decline to dangerous modernisms. The proper response to such histories is not to deny the strengths of these groups, but to draw their correctives into a larger framework shaped by the revelation of God in Christ, in Scripture and in the history of his people.

Closer to Home: A Notable Effort

The story of Christianity in America has been heavily influenced by both the positive and negative sides of Pietistic belief. The revival, which challenges sinners and calls the lukewarm to commitment, is the most prominent theme in our religious history. Sometimes this emphasis on religious experience has encouraged the effort to build Christian world views. Sometimes it has stood in the way. In very general terms, warm piety and hard thinking went well with each other in the early days of European settlement. From the late eighteenth century to fairly recent years, however, concentrated attention to the mind took a secondary place. The result was to make American Christian history nearly a model case to observe the benefits in promoting, and the perils in neglecting, the life of the mind.

Jonathan Edwards. Jonathan Edwards (1703-1758) provides a good example of how many things it is possible for an awakened believer to think about like a Christian. Edwards was a leader in the colonial revival of the 1730s and 1740s known as the Great Awakening. He was a New England minister who always insisted that a living spirituality was the one indispensable thing. Yet Edwards also realized how vital it was to struggle toward distinctly Christian views of the world.

Edwards was living through a period of changing world views and changing evaluations of God and humanity. Historians often describe this period as the age of Scientific Revolution. But the reality was even more comprehensive. Changes in scientific theories were only the most obvious signs of great alterations in general attitudes. By the time of Edwards, the conventions of the Enlightenment had come to prevail widely on the continent, in Great Britain and also in America. In his age, almost all thinkers of consequence, Christian or not, had come to assume that the fundamental reality was matter in motion and that fundamental truth depended on human apprehension. From these assumptions movements were arising to challenge intellectual traditions, some of them in philosophy, some in science, some in religion and some in politics.[11]

The intellectual accomplishment of Jonathan Edwards was his refusal to admit that these assumptions were in fact the starting points of thought. His work was important for his own time and for later Christians precisely because it dealt constantly with world views at their most basic level. Edwards refused to acknowledge that matter or the human perception of the world was the foundation of intellectual activity. And this refusal rested self-consciously on explicit Christian convictions. God was the source of reality; God was the source of truth; human intellect and the world itself were ever and always dependent on him. For Edwards, truth was not an abstract correspondence of our thinking with reality, but was rather "the consistency and agreement of our ideas with the ideas of God."[12]

This self-consciousness about world views grew out of Edwards's Christian beliefs. He felt that all the world belonged to God, who had brought it into existence originally and who sustained it each moment by his loving providence. He felt furthermore that humans were dependent on God's grace for the ability both to be truly virtuous and to understand the world correctly. To be sure, Edwards held that we can learn a great deal about ourselves and our world from those who do not honor God. But this knowledge is always secondary. Only a heart changed by God's grace will understand itself, God, the world of nature and the proper potential of human existence.

The comprehensiveness of Edwards's thought, just as much as

his desire to regard all questions from a distinctly Christian perspective, makes him unusual in American Christian history. Over a lifetime of unceasing intellectual labor, Edwards worked out Christian responses to many of the troubling issues of his day. These included matters in theology, where Edwards wrestled with the relationship between divine sovereignty and human freedom; in psychology, where he explored the components of genuine religious emotion; in philosophy, where he proposed ways of counteracting the drift toward scientific materialism; and in ethics, where he differentiated between prudential self-love and true virtue.

The structure of Edwards's thought was the same in each of these areas. The basis was always God's being and our understanding of God's actions through Scripture. Edwards was properly respectful of the human ability to understand nature, whether physical or human. But he also always denied that this natural knowledge was the highest or finest knowledge. That kind of understanding we receive through faith in Christ by God's grace. Edwards's efforts to think in comprehensive terms about the actual construction of world views enabled him to have a perspective on most of the major intellectual proposals of his day. The challenge he poses to later Christians lies partly in the actual conclusions which he reached. Even more, it lies in his effort to think about all the major dimensions of life distinctly as a Christian, from a Christian base, and with Christian principles.

Politics and Social Theory. Unfortunately for the legacy of Edwards, the one significant area in which he did the least work came to exert the most important influence on America. This was the area of politics and social theory. Edwards's theology, psychology, philosophy and ethics continued to influence New England Protestants for nearly a century. But the country at large was swept away in the meantime by the heady principles of the American Revolution. For a number of reasons, Edwards had not concentrated on politics as he had on other spheres of life. Unfortunately, almost no other Christians in colonial America were thinking about politics from distinctly Christian foundations either. The consequence was that the political values of the American Revolution reflected a very mixed set of influences: some Christian, some naturalistic and humanistic, some quite altruistic, some very self-seeking, some noble in their intents, some quite base in their effects, some clear-eyed and perceptive, some hopelessly befogged by the heated propaganda of the period. When this confused amalgam became the dominant factor in shaping the American world view during and after the Revolution, Edwards's careful insistence that all thinking must begin and end with God gradually faded away. The American Revolution taught people to trust themselves to fashion a new and better society. And although there was much room within such a world view for Christian values, the comprehensive Christian perspective of Edwards did not fit into it easily.[13]

Edwards's point of view did, nonetheless, continue to have considerable influence. It provided an ethical base for some of his followers to attack slavery as an offense against true virtue. It provided a vision of Christian life with a place for belief, emotions and the exercise of the will. It lent a moral tone to aspirations for the United States. And it remained a reservoir of serious Christian thinking to which small groups of later believers would return from time to time for challenge and reflection. Within the last fifty years the comprehensive range and depth of Edwards's thought have even received attention from secular scholars who are able to recognize the creativity with which he dealt with the important questions. It is even fair to say that at several of the major American universities one of the strongest Christian witnesses in recent decades has been Jonathan Edwards.

Edwards's intellectual career illustrates the power of Christian thinking when it is taken as a basis for the construction of world views. Edwards was not Godlike in his own thinking, and so he undoubtedly got some things wrong. But he did see clearly that if believers are to think like Christians, they must begin with the foundations of thought. He thought that to begin with natural laws and then work back somehow to God is reversing the appropriate order. Today, learning a little about Edwards and his thought may serve as an inspiration for believers to respond to the intellectual problems of our time with the comprehensive Christian purposes that this New England minister brought to the issues of his.

Active Revival but Intellectual Neglect

Two generations after Jonathan Edwards passed from the scene, American churches experienced their greatest period of revival and renewal. The Second Great Awakening from roughly 1795 to 1830 received its name because the movement shared many of the features of the colonial Great Awakening. But the Second Awakening did even more than the revival in the age of Edwards to revitalize Christian life in America. Only in its relative lack of concern for the mind can the Second Awakening be rated less highly than the first. But the consequences which flowed from the neglect of intellectual life in the Second Awakening pose a sobering lesson for modern believers. Stated most simply, it is that a lack of attention to the formation of world views undermined the long-term health of Christianity in the United States.

Post-Revolution. The state of religion in the country after the American Revolution was not good. Concern for creating a new nation, for populating the open lands west of the Appalachians, for overcoming the ravages of inflation and for staying clear of foreign entanglements left little room for spiritual life. In addition, a well-publicized attack on traditional Christianity convinced many that the old faith was not worth preserving. Led by heroes of the Revolution like Ethan Allen and Tom Paine, deists, who believed only in a mechanical or moral First Cause, called into question the need for a divine Savior. As a result of these varied influences, allegiance to the churches wavered. Less than ten per cent of the population actually belonged to local congregations, the lowest figure in the history of the country. And many areas on the frontier were entirely devoid of Christian influence.

Widespread evangelization, new life in the churches and cultural renewal came swiftly to both East and West.[14] On the western frontier (Kentucky, Tennessee and territories not yet states) the revival was promoted by Presbyterian, Baptist and Methodist itinerants. In the East it was led by several well-known ministers, like the president of Yale College, Timothy Dwight. Fervent preaching, careful attention to God's law, tender concern for the weak and despairing, forthright defense of the Bible—all of these contributed to a ground swell of Christian vitality which soon covered much of the country.

The permanent legacy of this revival was the great number of voluntary societies which arose in its wake. Traveling revivalists, concerned laypeople and regular preachers united to promote various Christian causes. Thus, in a very few years after the beginning of the awakening, special groups had come into existence to promote foreign missions, to distribute the Bible and other Christian literature, to liberate the slaves, to establish biblically based Sunday schools, to encourage temperance reform, to plan home missions, to reform prisons, to care for widows and orphans and to do many other Christian deeds. These societies helped greatly to spread the gospel and make the land a far more moral place.

The Loss of Christian Thinking. Nonetheless, there was a tiny cloud on the horizon. The Second Great Awakening, for all its positive points, did not lead to concerted effort in Christian thinking. This was, as it happens, not a particularly desperate problem at the time. Piety, spiritual fervor and ardent devotion seemed to be all that was needed to banish non-Christian ideas from the scene. Yet leaders of the awakening were mortgaging their own future. They followed most aspects of the Great Commandment, as recorded in Mark 12, loving the Lord with heart, strength and soul. But they did not succeed as well in loving the Lord with their minds.

Even before the Civil War, certain problems existed for American Christians which needed to be addressed from the perspective of comprehensive world views. Some of these seemed more secular in nature, some more obviously spiritual. But they all shared a common character as difficulties which could not be solved simply by the exercise of Christian good will or the fervent zeal of a revival. All required the kind of carefully thought-out solutions grounded in consistent approaches to the world that had marked the work of Thomas Aquinas, the leaders of the Reformation or Jonathan Edwards. But such approaches were largely lacking.

Problems included the nagging political conflict between Northern and Southern states which had festered behind the scenes since the days of the Constitution and which finally led to civil war. Somewhat less obvious were problems in society and economics. How would this new land react to the growing numbers of immigrants? Was it a genuinely free land or a land hospitable only to northern European Protestants? Even before the Civil War, outsiders from Catholic Ireland and from Asia had been made to feel unwelcome in "the land of the free." And this was to say nothing of the black population, which continued as a gross contradiction to the lofty sentiments of the Declaration of Independence. Did the American way of life have a place for you if you were black?

The most important economic questions dealt with the early growth of industrialization. What kinds of obligations did capital and labor owe to each other? How would the growth of large industries, first in textiles and then in railroads, affect community life or provisions for the disabled, aged or infirmed? Each of these questions, and many more like them, posed a potential threat to the Christian witness and public morality. Each of them was also the sort that could be answered only by those who had thought through principles of Scripture, who had struggled to see how the truths of creation, fall and redemption applied to groups as well as to individuals. Unfortunately, there was very little of such thinking. These problems developed pretty much under their own steam and received little specific attention from Christians wrestling with the foundations of thought and practice.

Science and the Bible. On intellectual questions more directly related to religious belief there was a similar intellectual nonchalance. Christian theologians gladly accepted results of the newer astronomy and geology, since they felt that such advances were compatible with a Christian understanding of the world. Most such thinkers readily adjusted earlier conclusions about the age of the earth, pushing their estimates back in time as a response to the work of the scientists. But there was little conceptual rigor in these accommodations between science and Scripture. It seemed the thing to do somehow, and little attention was given to principles which made such steps appropriate to, or dangerous for, the Christian understanding of the world. Later on, when scientific proposals that did not fit so easily into traditional understandings appeared, there were few guidelines concerning how best to sort out useful from harmful applications of the new science. A similar conclusion can be made about the meager efforts which American Christian leaders were making to stay abreast of discussions in Europe concerning the nature of the Bible.

The difficulty in all this was not so much that Christians lacked *immediate* solutions to these problems. The difficulty came rather in the fact that there was very scant encouragement to find *thorough* solutions to these issues. Little need was felt to exercise the mind for Christ in these areas since evangelism and fervent moral activism seemed to be so successful in meeting the church's immediate needs.

But eventually the chickens came home to roost.[15] After the Civil War, a sense of cultural and intellectual crisis grew rapidly. Evangelism continued powerfully, with much good being accomplished by well-known figures like Dwight L. Moody. But Christians also suffered many blows, and were pressed beyond their intellectual resources. Within a generation, the cities had mushroomed; older churches no longer seemed able to preserve a vital witness in these cities; immigration brought hordes of new Americans and many problems of social cohesion; mammoth factories sprang up and their owners achieved unrivaled influence in public life; freed slaves were forced back into inhumane conditions in the South and allowed a mere subsistence in the North; the Bible came increasingly under attack as a largely irrelevant mythological book; and new views in biology challenged both divine creation and the uniqueness of the human species.

Few Christian Answers. When Christians turned to their intellectual resources for dealing with these matters, they found that the cupboard was very nearly bare. Scripture, they believed, still had the answers to all of life's problems, but what were they? Who had been spending time thinking about these kinds of social and intellectual problems? Who had been devoting the energy to these issues that had been devoted to evangelism? The sad answer is that almost no one had been engaged in such a process of consistent Christian thinking.

As a result the Christian cause suffered. The effective evangelism and moral fervor of an earlier age had not been matched by comparable Christian attention to the mind. The consequences were sobering. A theological liberalism emerged which had little concern for traditional understandings of human sinfulness, God's grace and the supernatural work of Christ. A rival fundamentalism held on to these basic Christian truths, but fled from the problems of the wider world into fascination with inner spirituality or details of prophecy about the end times.[16] A secular spirit spread rapidly in the general culture. And the new city dwellers, the industrialized regions, and the university-trained became harder and harder to reach with the gospel.

It is no exaggeration to say that the process of secularization which has posed so many difficulties for Christians in our century is in considerable measure the result of Christians in the last century neglecting questions of the mind. A failure to balance evangelistic and reforming zeal with zeal for the intellect left the church as a whole unbalanced and eventually weakened its ability to cope with the particular problems of modern existence.

The Immediate Past

There are signs of hope in regard to the careful construction of world views. Believers are being informed more consistently that Christian world views cannot be simply veneered versions of current intellectual fashions. The theoretical and practical challenges of Marxism have contributed to this clearer perception. And so too has the secularization of the West. The drift of Western culture has posed especially complex problems for Christian thinking. On the one hand, there are many elements of this civilization that Christians rightly prize as gifts of God. On the other hand, there is in the West an ongoing temptation to simply classify as Christian the elements of our culture that are neutral or actually hostile to the faith.

In this situation many voices are now calling believers to think through current dilemmas with distinctively Christian foundations of thought. Not all of these agree concerning the solutions to our modern problems, but they do sound a united appeal to operate from Christian frameworks as we approach the world.

Catholic Intellectual Revival. Twentieth-century Catholic thinking has enjoyed two major periods of stimulation. The first came in a revival of Thomas Aquinas's thought in the first half of the century. Especially in America, leaders at Catholic colleges and universities used Thomistic insights to call on scholars to develop consistent Christian visions for education, life in a pluralistic society and world politics. Then the Second Vatican Council (1962-1965) opened Catholics to more intense interaction with modern thought generally. In the person of the present pope, John Paul II, we see in microcosm some of the fruits of this Catholic interest in the life of the mind. The pope had been trained at centers of Neo-Thomistic influence, he had his ideas tested through life in officially atheistic Poland, and he had himself done major academic projects on Catholic mysticism and modern phenomenology. Protestants will, of course, continue to question many specific aspects of Catholic teaching. But at the same time they should be able to recognize that the mind of Catholicism presents a forceful Christian world view. As the pope speaks out on pressing modern problems—whether warfare, the dissolution of the family, evangelization or economic justice—he illustrates the potential for vitality in modern Catholic thinking.[17]

A similar vitality is also present among some of England's recent Christian spokesmen. Early in the century G. K. Chesterton urged believers to critically examine the supposed triumphs of modern life to see if we may not have sold our souls for mere political innovation. Much the same message, with much the same rhetorical verve, is prominent in the work of Malcolm Muggeridge. Although Chesterton and Muggeridge both eventually joined the Catholic Church, their sharp critique of modern evils and their penetrating presentation of alternative Christian visions have been of great benefit to believers of all sorts on both sides of the Atlantic.[18]

C. S. Lewis and American Evangelicals. Even more influential have been the efforts of the Oxford literary scholar, C. S. Lewis. In essays on a multitude of topics and in a number of seminal books, Lewis exemplified a mind which sought to reflect divine as well as temporal realities. Lewis's numerous readers, followers and successors received from him the message that it is respectable to think like a Christian in the twentieth century, but even more than being respectable, it is absolutely essential if human dignity and religious faith are to receive their due.[19]

American evangelicals in the generation after World War 2 have also expressed a need for more distinctively Christian approaches to the intellectual and practical crises of our day. A leader in these efforts is Carl F. H. Henry, theologian and ethicist, who has challenged believers to cultivate the mind seriously, not only on topics related immediately to Scripture and Christian living, but also on questions of science, values and other general matters. Many teachers in Christian colleges and many Christians in higher education at large, as well as several forceful evangelists and popular apologists, have joined in appealing for self-consciously Christian evaluations of our modern situation.[20]

A Challenge for the Future

Not everything, however, is sweetness and light. Americans are still prone to take a short cut when faced with complex intellectual or cultural problems. The pattern of snappy, largely unthinking responses to such crises is so well ingrained that we are often prone to react rather than to think when faced with a troubling issue. Enough examples remain of Christians forsaking careful reflection for a quick fix of one sort or another to keep us realistic about the nature of our successes.

If history can be any guide, we can conclude that Christian thinking requires the same serious attention as evangelism and personal spirituality. The mind is a gift from God. It may be used for his glory, neglected to its waste or abused idolatrously. In our American history, as in the fuller history of the church, we have many encouraging examples of how faithful use of the intellect has advanced the kingdom of God. And there are many examples of the opposite. No special claims are made by Christians for the mind. At the same time Christians recognize that the mind too may bring praise to its Maker. To construct Christian world views and to act for Christ in daily existence on the basis of those world views is a high calling. History shows two things about such a calling: that by God's grace it can be done, but also that it is never an easy task.

3
A Christian View of the Physical World

Joseph Spradley

How does a Christian view of the physical world differ from current scientific views? All scientists, Christian and non-Christian alike, usually agree on the content of scientific knowledge. Physicists see the world in terms of interacting forces and wavelike particles. Chemists explore the changing arrangements of matter and energy that produce stable molecular configurations. Biologists view the earth as a fragile sphere of interdependent life forms constantly evolving and adjusting to a changing environment. Astronomers observe our galaxy of billions of stars rushing away from billions of other galaxies in an ever-expanding universe.

A Christian world view welcomes this growing vision of the cosmos, but seeks a broader perspective and raises questions beyond the limits of science. What is the meaning and purpose of this awesome spectacle and how can we account for its order and source? Who are we and what is the significance of human consciousness in this vast universe? Why does human society experience evil and how can we know what is right and true? These are metaphysical and moral questions that go beyond the competence of science. My goal is to assess the prospects for a Christian view of these concerns and to outline the principles and practice of such a view.

Prospects for a Christian View of Nature

A Christian world view understands the universe as the creation of an all-wise and powerful God who has made us in his image and has revealed himself in Christ and the Bible. In such a world view nature and Scripture provide complementary revelations so that science and theology can be related by mutual respect and support. However, any effort to develop a Christian view of the physical world is challenged by the widespread belief in a fundamental conflict between science and religion.[1]

Opposition to a Christian View of Nature. Science and Christianity have not always enjoyed a positive relationship. It is often claimed that the early church fathers retarded the progress of science and blocked its development for more than a millennium.[2] In the Renaissance, the Copernican theory that the sun rather than the earth is the center of the universe became a threat to Catholic theologians, culminating in the trial and censure of Galileo. Although the new heliocentric view of the universe was finally established and accepted within a Christian tradition, it eventually led to a mechanization of the universe that seemed to make Christianity irrelevant. In the nineteenth century the Darwinian controversy over the origin of species renewed the basic theme of conflict between science and theology.[3]

The success of science has led to various attempts to develop a scientific world view in which all knowledge conforms to scientific standards. Logical positivism based its claim to knowledge on empirical verification and rejected metaphysical and theological statements as empirically unverifiable and therefore meaningless. Value judgments were also considered devoid of observable data and therefore purely emotive.

Naturalistic humanism also lays claim to a scientific world view but tries to retain values. However, it limits them to what has value for humanity as the measure of all things.[4] But since human beings are viewed as entirely a part and product of nature, human uniqueness is lost and it is difficult to see how the evil generated by natural processes can be overcome. Furthermore, insofar as these kinds of scientism seek to reduce everything to scientific explanations they end up dehumanizing persons by disallowing other kinds of human knowledge and insight.[5]

The inadequacies of scientism suggest the need for a more comprehensive and unifying world view within which to interpret the physical world and the proper role of science in it. The tendency toward scientific specialization leads to a fragmentation of knowledge and a multiplication of facts and theories assumed to be value-free. Under the influence of logical positivism, values and religion were relegated to arbitrary and irrational preferences. The loss of purpose and value in science leads to a sense of meaninglessness and removes the safeguards against the exploitation of nature and pollution of the environment.[6]

But a Christian world view offers the possibility of a unifying perspective for seeing life whole and finding meaning in each part. The action of God in Christ restores human purpose and hope. Such a world view is needed to guide thought and action and to restore a sense of responsibility for God's creation.

Opportunities for a Christian View of Nature. New possibilities for a closer relation between science and religion have developed over the last three decades with the decline of logical positivism under the influence of a new evaluation of the history of science. This historical analysis of scientific concepts in their context of discovery demonstrated that observational data are shaped by the conceptual scheme of the observer and thus are "theory-laden."[7] Subjective factors and value judgments enter into the selection of data, how they are recorded and related to other data, and how they are interpreted and applied.

Thomas Kuhn carried this analysis a step further in his study of scientific revolutions.[8] Kuhn distinguished between "normal science" during periods when a particular paradigm is widely accepted as a model or ideal of explanation, and periods of revolution when there is no agreement between competing paradigms. For example, the Ptolemaic system of astronomy was the accepted paradigm throughout the Middle Ages; but for several decades during the Renaissance at least two paradigms were locked in competition: the Ptolemaic geocentric system and the Copernican heliocentric system.[9] Such paradigms determine the kinds of problems scientists pursue, as well as the facts they consider relevant. The revolution which occurs in a shift from one paradigm to another involves changing values and commitments to a new pattern or perspective.

The study of historical revolutions revealed science as it actually is, showing its continually changing concepts which depend on elements of a larger world view including values, attitudes and commitments. Biblical values have had a strong influence on attitudes toward nature throughout most of history, and these biblical values and attitudes are the primary basis for a Christian view of the physical world.

Origins of a Christian View of Nature. In considering the biblical basis for a Christian view of the physical world it is important to recognize that the Scriptures were intended to teach theological truths rather than scientific ideas, which are within the mandate of human responsibility. Any attempt to show a precise correspondence between science and Scripture will be defeated by the changing nature of human scientific concepts. A more fruitful approach involves a cultural and historical interpretation.

For example, the Genesis creation narrative is difficult to interpret chronologically since the earth and plants appear on the third day while the sun and moon are not mentioned until the fourth day (Gen 1:11-19). Cultural considerations suggest the possibility that this ordering was intended as a rejection of Babylonian idolatry. The Babylonians deified nature; the sun and moon together with the planets were among their chief deities. The seven days of the week were named after these planets, thus designating each day for worship of the corresponding planetary deity.

The biblical account avoids the usual Babylonian names of the sun and moon. It negates their identification with gods by referring to them as the "greater" and "lesser" lights (Gen 1:16) and gives them a reduced priority in the order of their description. The seven-day week is thus given a new significance symbolizing God's control and ordering of his creation. In this view the days of creation provide a ritual order for celebrating God's creation rather than a scientific chronology.[10]

The primary purpose of the creation account is not to offer a substitute for science, but to call God's people away from idolatry to worship the Creator rather than his creation. This distinction between nature and God was an important prerequisite to a scientific understanding of nature.[11]

The inability of Babylonian and Egyptian civilizations to think scientifically despite their technical abilities can be correlated with their basic attitudes toward nature. In these early civilizations both humans and gods were part of nature. History and society were integrally related to cosmologies which connected humanity with the cosmos. Annual floods and celestial motions combined with mythological traditions and deities to provide the framework for societal cohesion. Humans were controlled by nature so long as they perceived it as an extension of society and an embodiment of deities to be placated.

Scientific curiosity and creativity require the disenchantment of the physical world and the removal of its terror. Such a result was initiated by the biblical view of creation which for the first time established a separation of nature from God and made it a matter of human responsibility. The doctrine of creation provides the principles for a Christian view of the physical world, which will be considered next.

Principles of a Christian View of Nature

A Christian view of nature is based primarily on the biblical doctrine of creation.[12] This doctrine is not confined to the early chapters of Genesis but permeates the Scriptures with its unequivocal proclamation that God is the Maker of heaven and earth. In contrast to mythological cosmogonies, God is not generated out of some kind of primal chaos, but he is prior to every part of his creation. All things came into being by his will rather than through cosmic struggle. The world is not subject to the conflicting forces of immanent gods which must be placated but is under the control of one God who created it by his power and for his purpose.

The attitudes and principles contained in this doctrine can be correlated with three basic aspects of science. First, the reality and goodness of creation provide a basis and motivation for experimental science. Second, the order and intelligibility of nature are essential for theoretical science. Third, the purpose and meaning of creation encourage the development of applied science. Each of these principles can be contrasted with Greek attitudes to show how a Christian view transcends the limitations of Greek science, as well as similar limitations in Oriental science.

Creation Is Real and Good. Experimental science, in both laboratory and field work, is based on an affirmative attitude toward the physical world. The goodness and reality of nature are explicit in the Bible and support the observational and experimental activities of science. The first verse of the Bible establishes the existence of the basic categories of physical reality: "In the beginning God created the heavens and the earth" (Gen 1:1). Thus time, space and matter find their reality grounded in creation.[13]

We can also enjoy an attitude of delight in the goodness of nature. Six times in the first chapter of Genesis the statement is repeated that each addition to the created order is good, concluding with a seventh affirmation that "God saw everything that he had made, and behold, it was very good" (Gen 1:31). Even after the fall of man and the resulting curse (Gen 3:17) the goodness of creation is reaffirmed: "For everything created by God is good, and nothing is to be rejected if it is received with thanksgiving" (1 Tim 4:4).

Because the physical world is revealed as good it is worthy of detailed and devoted study. Because it is real such efforts will not be irrelevant or illusory. However, the goodness of creation does not imply a realm of perfection. For one thing, nature is temporal and must never be considered as ultimate (Heb 1:10-12). The world is also a place of human probation and judgment (Gen 3:16-19). The earth with its thorns and thistles is not evil in itself, but it does not function for humanity as God originally intended. Evil is an intruder in a world that is otherwise by nature good.

Saint Augustine suggests that the goodness of a thing must not be judged by our convenience or comfort, but with respect to its own nature and use.[14] Thus the psalmist speaks of "wine to gladden the heart of man, oil to make his face shine, and bread to strengthen man's heart" (Ps 104:15). Jesus delights in the birds of the air and lilies of the field (Mt 6:26-28). Such an attitude is possible for anyone who recognizes that this is his Father's world.

Greek science was hindered by the Platonic view of matter as chaotic and imperfect, receiving only a semblance of order from eternal and unchanging Forms. Knowledge for Plato involved rational contemplation of the real world of eternal Forms, while observation and experience of the material world led only to opinion and illusion. As a result of this dualism Greek science tended to focus on the celestial realm of perfection more than on the terrestrial realm of imperfection and change.

The Greek intellectual tradition also tended to concentrate on rational speculation and shun physical manipulation, leaving manual labor for artisans and slaves. In later Greek thought Neo-Platonism superimposed a hierarchical order on the world. A great chain-of-being stretched from God down to matter at the bottom, which was associated with evil. A new evaluation of matter and labor was required before the Greek aversion to experimental science could be overcome.

Christian theology emerged in a Greek world but showed marked contrast with Greek thought in its doctrines of creation, Incarnation and resurrection, together with their associated values and attitudes toward the material world and manual labor. In the Incarnation of God's Son "the Word became flesh and dwelt among us, full of grace and truth; we have beheld his glory, glory as of the only Son from the Father" (Jn 1:14). In this event the perfection of Christ was revealed in a material body. Work in his father's carpenter shop further affirmed both the value of material objects and physical labor.

Paul commanded his followers to work with their hands (1 Thess 4:11). In his sermon at Athens Paul began with the doctrine of creation, denying the traditional Greek dichotomy between celestial and terrestrial: "The God who made the world and everything in it, being Lord of heaven and earth, does not live in shrines made by man" (Acts 17:24). Paul stirred the greatest reaction among his Greek audience by ending his sermon with a reference to the resurrection (Acts 17:32). The sharpest contrast between Greek and Christian attitudes toward the physical world relate to their respective future hopes.[15] The Greeks saw death as escape from the material body by an immortal soul, while the Christian hope is the resurrection of the body and God's future kingdom (1 Cor 15).

The Greek tradition of learning, modified and enriched by Christian thought, was transmitted to Western Europe during the Middle Ages by the monastic movement. Early in the sixth century St. Benedict established a monastic order with a rule of life placing equal emphasis on learning and labor. Each of the monks participated in farming and housekeeping along with their scholarly work, thus weakening the Greek dichotomy.

In the thirteenth century St. Francis of Assisi established the Franciscan order with its emphasis on poverty and joy among God's creatures. He called the animals his "brothers and sisters," and emphasized new attitudes of appreciation for the natural world. The Franciscan tradition was carried into the new university world at Oxford by Robert Grosseteste and Roger Bacon, among the first to emphasize an experimental approach in science. The nominalist movement in the fourteenth century reacted against Greek universals and stimulated a new interest in the particulars of experience in the material world.

These Christian attitudes and values developed in the Middle Ages are evident in the pioneers of the scientific revolution. Francis Bacon urged scholars to collect facts as the basis for theories. His inductive method became an ideal for empirical science based on observation and experiment. Galileo also emphasized the new empirical approach to science, but with a greater appreciation for the importance of mathematical theory. His telescope observations turned the tide in favor of the Copernican theory, and his experiments on motion provided the basis for the laws of Newton.

However, more than inductive methods were needed for the success of the scientific revolution. Empirical science must be guided by theory to aid in the selection and interpretation of data, and to ensure that observed regularities are more than accidental or meaningless occurrences. Theory in science is also supported by biblical attitudes and values.

Nature Is Ordered and Intelligible. Theoretical science, both mathematical and descriptive, is made possible by the order and intelligibility of the universe. The wisdom of God ensures that his creation will have an intrinsic regularity and order, validating the rational and logical dimensions of science. The regularity of nature is based on more than experience of past events and an inductive assumption about the future. It is grounded in the faithfulness of God who created and sustains the universe. The laws of nature have their source in the nature of God. Order in the physical world is the product of divine wisdom: "O LORD, how manifold are thy works! In wisdom hast thou made them all" (Ps 104:24).

Regularity and uniformity are made explicit in numerous biblical references. God promised Noah the regularity of "seedtime and harvest, cold and heat, summer and winter, day and night" (Gen 8:22). Job refers to a "decree for the rain, and a way for the lightning" (Job 28:26) and Jeremiah speaks of the "fixed order of the moon and the stars" (Jer 31:35). Biblical monotheism also implies the unity of the created order in which natural laws apply uniformly throughout the universe.

The doctrine of creation also offers assurance that the created order will be intelligible to human reason. It reveals that the universe has a design in which patterns can be discovered. The biblical affirmation that "God created man in his own image, in the image of God he created him" (Gen 1:27), suggests that the order of creation and the laws of logic are reflected in human creativity and intelligence. It is also important to remember that we are a part of nature (Gen 2:7) and thus finite as well as fallen creatures (Gen 3:6-7). But the ability to think God's thoughts about the universe is reaffirmed by the psalmist even after the Fall: "Great are the works of the LORD, studied by all who have pleasure in them" (Ps 111:2). The prophet Isaiah invites us to reason even about our sins (Is 1:18). Though rational inquiry is limited by human fallibility and finiteness (1 Cor 13:12), the Christian view has faith that reason is reliable and creation is comprehensible.

The Greek vision of order in the world lacked an adequate concept of creation to recognize the reality of matter and to be freed from bondage to rational Forms. For the Greeks in the Platonic tradition, order was only partially and imperfectly realized in the material world, and could only be apprehended by rational contemplation of eternal Forms. Aristotle viewed order in terms of inherent purposive Forms within nature but it was never completely or perfectly realized. In both views the material aspects of the world were merely accidental, while the rational Forms were intelligible by direct intellectual vision. Thus Greek science did not trace the contingent and observable material causes, but searched for formal structures or essences through rational intuition of the Forms.

By contrast, in the Christian view the created order cannot be deduced from rational Forms, but is contingent on God's will and can only be discovered by observation of material relations. If the order of things cannot be determined by logical deduction, then we must examine them to see how they actually are ordered.[16] Thus theoretical science must combine with empirical science to discover the contingent order of creation, since the regularity of nature is a gift of God rather than a logical necessity.

Correlated with contingency is the affirmation of the freedom of the Creator's will to act in his creation and to reveal himself through it. This is reaffirmed in the Christian doctrines of providence and revelation. God continues his creative activity in sustaining the universe and providing for his creatures, especially through the work of Christ: "For by him . . . all things consist" (Col 1:16-17 KJV). He "upholds all things by the word of His power" (Heb 1:3 NASB).

Nature is a source of revelation of God's providential faithfulness and power: "He did not leave himself without witness, for he did good and gave you from heaven rains and fruitful seasons, satisfying your hearts with food and gladness" (Acts 14:17). For "ever since the creation of the world his invisible nature, namely, his eternal power and deity, has been clearly perceived in the things that have been made" (Rom 1:20). For the psalmist the order and intelligibility of the world are clearly revealed in nature: "The heavens are telling of the glory of God; and their expanse is declaring the work of His hands. Day to day pours forth speech, And night to night reveals knowledge" (Ps 19:1-2 NASB).

During the Middle Ages and the Reformation further implications of the doctrine of creation were developed in support of rational inquiry and theoretical science. Thomas Aquinas in the thirteenth century is especially noteworthy for adapting Aristotelian science within a consistent Christian understanding of creation. Even though much of Aristotle's hierarchical cosmology was later rejected, the emphasis of Thomistic theology on the intelligibility of nature and the importance of reason contributed to a growing faith in the possibility of science. The modern philosophical appraisal of Whitehead recognizes this medieval contribution:

> When we compare this tone of thought in Europe with the attitude of other civilizations when left to themselves, there seems but one source for its origin. It must come from the medieval insistence on the rationality of God, conceived as with the personal energy of Jehovah and with the rationality of a Greek philosopher. Every detail was supervised and ordered: the search into nature could only result in the vindication of the faith in rationality.[17]

The Reformers, especially Calvin, emphasized the freedom of God's will and the contingency of creation.[18] Whereas natural law for Aquinas was part of God's wise and rational sovereignty, Reformed theology related law to God's power and providence. The idea that all creatures were dependent on God's power undercut the hierarchical chain-of-being and contributed to a more egalitarian view of the material world. The Reformed concept of the priesthood of all believers before God supported a new confidence in individual interpretation of Scripture and the intelligibility of God's revelation in nature without reference to scholastic authority.

The Christian emphasis on order and reason is evident in the theoretical work during the scientific revolution of men like Descartes and Newton. Descartes applied new methods of mathematics and logic to science and even attempted to deduce laws of motion from the attributes of God. His conception of a universal deductive system anticipated the future structure of physical science but underestimated the importance of experimentation.

A more balanced application of both empirical and theoretical science led to the success of the Newtonian synthesis. The law of universal gravitation was developed from a theoretical analysis of the empirical generalizations of Galileo and Kepler. It demonstrated the amazing order and unity of the world, accounting precisely for motions throughout the heavens and on earth by a single natural law. Newton saw this as evidence for God's creating and sustaining power:

> This most beautiful system of the sun, planets, and comets, could only proceed from the counsel and dominion of an intelligent and powerful Being. And if the fixed stars are the centres of other like systems, these, being formed by the like wise counsel, must be all subject to the dominion of One. . . . This Being governs all things, not as the soul of the world, but as Lord over all.[19]

The Newtonian synthesis of the laws of motion established a unified vision of the universe. It was now possible to apply the new scientific ideas and methods to the needs of society in a systematic and sustained way. This did not happen suddenly, but was recognized as a valid responsibility consistent with a Christian view, especially within the Puritan tradition.

History and Culture Have Meaning and Purpose. Applied science and technology are supported and encouraged by the creation mandate and its suggestion that history has meaning and purpose. This faith that human progress is both possible and important is based on the first command given by God to Adam and Eve: "And God blessed them, and God said to them, 'Be fruitful and multiply, and fill the earth and subdue it' " (Gen 1:28). Being created in the image of God ensures the creative and rational powers to exercise this responsibility. Neither sin nor grace cancels this creation mandate. It is reaffirmed after the Fall by the psalmist who declares, "Thou hast given him dominion over the works of thy hands" (Ps 8:6). It is repeated in the light of grace which helps to fulfill it:

> What is man that thou art mindful of him,

> or the son of man, that thou carest for him?
> Thou didst make him for a little while lower than the angels,
> thou has crowned him with glory and honor,
> putting everything in subjection under his feet. (Heb 2:6-8)

The doctrine of creation teaches that nature is not divine but is God's handiwork assigned to human responsibility for its care and protection: "The Lord God took the man and put him in the Garden of Eden to work it and take care of it" (Gen 2:15 NIV). Though we are a part of nature we are also set apart from nature and can live in the world free from enslavement to nature but responsible for it. The exercise of dominion is clearly distinguished from selfish exploitation by the call to responsible stewardship consistent with the intentions of the Creator.[20] Our distinction from nature and acceptance of dominion is what makes us human and is the basis for culture and civilization even though corrupted by sin.

The purpose and meaning of historical existence within the natural order also follow from the doctrine of creation and provide motivation and significance for science and technology. In the Greek view the transitory events of history could not give life permanent significance and meaning. Instead they were derived from the perfection of order and harmony. But in the world of change this could only be approximated by the orderly perfection of recurrence. The Hellenic mind perceived time as circular since a recurring cycle reduces change and history to a permanent pattern of harmony. This cyclical view of time is antithetical to human purposes and meaning since no goals can be achieved without vanishing again. If history is just an endless process of repetition, then no vocation can have lasting significance, and real progress is not possible.

The defeat of this deadly concept of circular time was one of the most important developments of Christian thought and Western culture, ending the temporal meaninglessness and pessimism of the ancient world.[21] The biblical understanding of history can be traced back to the Hebrew view of the exodus from Egypt, but it had its most complete formulation by Saint Augustine early in the fifth century. His concept of linear history is based on both creation and redemption. God created time with a beginning and an end, so its moments are unrepeatable and meaningful as they move toward a final goal. The eternal God sent Christ into the world to save us for an eternal destiny, relating time and eternity by this redemptive act rather than by recurring cycles. The redemption of human beings introduces new and eternally significant events into history. Augustine's two great works, the *Confessions* and *The City of God*, vividly illustrate both the personal history of the individual and the larger history of the human race as purposeful and meaningful.[22]

The Reformation doctrine of vocation applied this linear view of history to human responsibility before God. Both Calvin and Luther insisted that "secular" vocations were as important as "religious" callings and that it is possible to serve God in any honest and useful job.[23] Calvinism encouraged diligent work and thrifty habits in worldly duties as a way of promoting the general welfare and glorifying God. This "Protestant ethic" was especially endorsed by Puritanism and applied to scientific work.[24] This was reinforced by attitudes of self-restraint, simplicity and diligence. The study of nature was divinely sanctioned since it would reveal God's handiwork and exemplify orderly activity. The Puritans believed science could work for the glory of God and the benefit of society.

A secularized version of the Christian view of historical purpose emerged in the eighteenth century as the idea of progress. The success of science opened up the prospect of indefinite improvement of this life by application of human reason, slowly displacing the Christian vision of God's will and kingdom. The idea of progress was a perversion of the Christian doctrine of redemption with a new faith in human goodness and the efficacy of reason. The industrial revolution was the outward expression of this faith as it took on a more materialistic emphasis in the nineteenth century. As technological developments improved the outward conditions of life, the idea of progress and faith in applied science were reinforced, but too often without a sense of stewardship to protect against exploitation.

The principles of a Christian view of the physical world described above show how the attitudes and values supporting the various components of a healthy scientific perspective are drawn from the biblical doctrine of creation. These convictions are not found in nature as such but are matters of faith worked out over centuries of medieval and Reformation thought and given expression by the founders of modern science, many of whom were avowedly Christian. This faith gives light to see that the world is good and beautiful and worthy of the efforts of experimental science. Here also is the conviction that the Creator has ordered the universe and reveals it to patient inquiry, confirming the vision of theoretical science. And here is motivation and purpose for applied science to seek the advancement of human welfare with responsibility and wisdom. A brief evaluation of how these principles should be put into practice will help to show the relevance of a Christian world view for science.

Practicing a Christian View of Nature

Christians living in the contemporary world should not take for granted the successes of science nor ignore its negative influences. The creation mandate has applications for all Christians as they view the physical world and experience the benefits and burdens of modern science. Three aspects of practicing a Christian world view in relation to science will now be considered. First, the creation mandate calls for a creative response. Second, the theories and ideas of science require critical evaluation. And third, constructive efforts are needed in the exercise of responsible stewardship. These practical dimensions involve and illustrate the principles and values discussed above.

Creative Appreciation of Nature. A creative view of the physical world is an appropriate response to express appreciation for God's creation and to exercise our God-given creativity in seeking to understand and order nature for good ends. That the creation is good requires us to value and appreciate it. That it is ordered and intelligible calls for creative responsibility to study and care for it. God's example of creativity is evident all around us (Is 40:21-31). It is manifested by the gift of each new moment of time. Science offers an opportunity to celebrate God's creativity, to join the rest of creation in praising him (Ps 148) and to praise him the more intelligently by learning of his greatness and glory in nature: "Praise Him in His mighty expanse. Praise Him for His mighty deeds; Praise Him according to His excellent greatness" (Ps 150:1-2 NASB).

True appreciation is not passive, but rather it is creatively active. Science is more than a collection of facts and information about nature. It requires the exercise of human creativity. Artists do more than merely copy what they see; they select, interpret and create. In a similar way the scientist seeks to correlate data and create unifying concepts to exhibit the order and unity of nature. God created the animals, but he brought them to Adam to be named: "And whatever the man called a living creature, that was its name. And the man gave names to all the cattle, and to the birds of the sky, and to every beast of the field" (Gen 2:19-20 NASB). The Hebrew concept of naming is a truly creative act, and Adam's task was perhaps no less significant than the great efforts of biological classification by such men as Aristotle and Linnaeus.

Creative activity in ordering nature is the first step in exercising dominion and stewardship to "fill the earth, and subdue it; and rule over . . . every living thing" (Gen 1:28 NASB). Civilizations advance as they carry out this cultural and creational mandate. We have been given responsibility to cultivate and protect the earth which requires all the creative skills of applied science and technology. This practice of creativity requires both caution and confidence in the abilities and tools God has given. We are responsible for the consequences of our efforts as well as for our accomplishments.

The concept of an expanding universe in modern cosmology demonstrates both divine and human creativity. The discovery of a dynamic, changing universe reveals God's creative activity. Even before it was discovered that the galaxies are rapidly receding from each other, Einstein's theory of general relativity had predicted this expansion. But he had resisted the idea because it pointed to an original creation event and a more active God than he preferred. Accumulating evidence supporting the idea of an explosive creation and continuing expansion has disturbed others also: "For the scientist who has lived by his faith in the power of reason the story ends like a bad dream. He has scaled the mountains of ignorance; he is about to conquer the highest peak; as he pulls himself over the final rock, he is greeted by a band of theologians who have been there for centuries."[25]

At the end of the nineteenth century, when the laws of classical physics seemed complete in what appeared to be a static universe, one physicist suggested that all that remained for science was to improve the accuracy of existing measurements. The twentieth century has discovered an expanding universe of God's continuing creation together with the exploding knowledge of human creativity in investigating the physical world. The implications of this knowledge are difficult to grasp and must come under the critical scrutiny of a Christian world view.

Critical Evaluation of Science. The need for a critical view of theories about the physical world in modern science can be illustrated by a brief evaluation of some of its major concepts and their cultural interpretations since the beginning of the scientific revolution. The Copernican hypothesis led to the first serious clash between science and the church, and the eventual collapse of the medieval synthesis. It is a good example of how a new scientific view can challenge theological ideas. If the earth revolves around the sun, the stars should show an apparent annual shift in position which could not be observed in the sixteenth century nor for nearly three hundred years after. Copernicus's answer to this lack of empirical evidence was to suggest that the stars were at such vast distances that the earth's motion relative to the stars was negligible. As a result the universe came to be viewed as infinite and the earth was displaced from its center.

Although our place in the universe was questioned and Thomistic theology was challenged, new possibilities for theological renewal also emerged.[26] By denying the legitimacy of applying spatial terms to heaven and hell the spiritual dimension of religion was clarified. The new vision of an infinite universe added new meaning to the power and majesty of God. The development of the heliocentric system by Galileo and Kepler revealed a new mathematical order in the world, but also initiated a trend toward a quantitative and impersonal view of nature.

The Newtonian synthesis of physical laws also had positive and negative results from a Christian perspective. It introduced a new vision of the uniformity of nature, but culminated in a mechanical view of the world and a deistic separation of God from creation. At first the success of mechanistic science seemed to support an argument for God's design revealed in the structure of the universe. However, the emphasis on causal mechanisms resulted in the view of deism that God was the first cause in creating the world machine, but left it to run on its own.

Eventually even the need for a first cause was rejected, and scientists such as Laplace decided that the hypothesis of God was unnecessary. He universalized the cause-effect argument to claim that all future events are completely determined by their past history and the laws of motion. In this deterministic view the world was reduced to matter and motion and even human freedom was denied. This mechanistic reductionism saw humans as machines and matter as the ultimate reality devoid of purpose and meaning. It is clear that differing world views interpret the results of science in different ways, seeing in the same facts either design or despair.

The romantic movement of the nineteenth century reacted against the mechanistic view of a dead universe, but reduced God to the level of nature. The study of energy processes and developmental biology began to focus on change and growth in nature. The transcendent God of deism was rejected in favor of an immanent God involved in natural processes and evolving with the course of history. This confusion of God with nature and historical processes led to pantheistic ideas and nature idolatry.

These tendencies can be seen in the Darwinian theory of evolution which completed the conquest of naturalistic science, subjugating human life to natural laws which were extrapolated to provide a purely naturalistic account of human origins. The scientific faith in naturalism conflicts with theism, but evolutionary theory itself is acceptable if it isn't universalized and if human uniqueness is not surrendered.[27] This would seem to require some kind of special creative act in relation to human origins as suggested by the

Genesis account (Gen 2:7). Although Darwin undermined older views of teleology based on design, a reformulated teleological natural theology has been developed by F. R. Tennant and others to account for the coordination and interconnectedness of a world in which evolution can occur.[28] They argue for theism based on evidence such as the congruence between the human mind and the rationality of the world, the ubiquity of beauty and the presence of conditions supporting human values.

An alternative to the mechanistic particle model began to emerge in the nineteenth century with the development of energy and field concepts. The doctrine of conservation of energy emphasized the functioning of an entire system instead of just its parts, and Maxwell provided a complete theory of electricity and magnetism in terms of continuous fields permeating all of space. Both of these theories emphasized interdependent relationships rather than independent particles, eliminating the priority of matter and yielding a more unified and holistic view of physical reality.

Relativity and quantum theory are the two major physical theories of the twentieth century. They provide the most serious challenge to mechanistic science and introduce the possibility of a new scientific world view more congenial to Christian faith. Although these theories have been used to support various forms of relativism, idealism and positivism, such applications have been increasingly repudiated.[29]

Einstein's theory of relativity used electromagnetic concepts to radically revise Newtonian mechanical ideas in favor of field concepts. Relativity has destroyed the mechanistic assumption of an objectively detached observer. The fundamental properties of nature were found to depend on their relationship to the observer and are interrelated in a new unity between space, time, matter and energy, reflecting the unity and interdependence of the biblical view (Eph 4:1-16; Col 1:16-17).

The quantum theory of matter further revised classical mechanics with the wave concept of particles and its interpretation in terms of probabilities. Strict cause-effect mechanisms were replaced by statistical relationships and predictions. This led to Heisenberg's uncertainty principle which set an irreducible limit on the precision of measurements and revealed the extent to which the interaction between an observing subject and the observed object is unavoidable. The discovery of antimatter in 1932, including processes of particle creation and mutual annihilation, demonstrated the ephemeral and energistic nature of matter. In quantum theory the causal mechanisms and individual particles of classical mechanics dissolve into a complex system of interdependent relationships. Modern physics offers little support to either reductionism or determinism, but reinforces the holistic emphasis of a Christian view (Acts 17:24-28).

Christians must always resist the tendency to absolutize scientific ideas and models by a careful and critical evaluation to avoid the dangers of idolatry, rationalism and reductionism. The mechanical model leads too easily to materialism, determinism and a deistic view of God separated from creation. Developmental and process ideas often degenerate into naturalism, idealism and pantheistic conceptions of God in nature. Relativity and quantum theory have been used to support relativism and positivism. However, many of the concepts of science can contribute to a Christian view of the physical world if kept in a proper perspective.

Constructive Participation in the World. A constructive view of scientific theories is needed to determine the possible contributions of science to a Christian world view and to guide our participation as stewards of God's creation. Scientific ideas can reveal the glory of God in the unity and order of nature if they are not reduced to narrow scientisms that deny his activity or existence. Scientific discoveries often modify established ideas and introduce new ways of seeing the world. Modern physics has demonstrated that mechanistic science can no longer supply the ultimate conceptions of physical reality but is only a partial and approximate description of nature. When overextended it led to a separation of object from subject, matter from mind, fact from value and science from religion. The emerging vision of the unity and interrelatedness of nature in a dynamic, changing universe offers new possibilities for eliminating mechanistic dichotomies and restoring the relational and personal emphases of a Christian world view (1 Cor 12:12-27).

The development of modern science reaffirms the importance of persons in scientific observations and discoveries. Science is a creative human activity. Subjective involvement in observing nature reveals the personal elements in our finite historical existence.[30] All data is theory-laden and facts require human interpretation. Thus observation is active rather than passive, selecting on the basis of subjective aims and values. Knowledge arises from neither subject nor object alone, but from their mutual interaction in the processes of inquiry.

Since science requires personal involvement and choices based on values, its success depends on responsible participation. The myth of determinism is contradicted by the fact that even the act of observing requires the free choice and interpretation of an active observer. Christianity emphasizes the freedom and dignity of persons as valuing and responsible agents, which are necessary conditions for the conduct of science itself.

Quantum theory also supports the Christian view of an open universe. Causal relations exist between probabilities at the atomic level, but these do not completely determine observable events since measurements give only one value out of many possibilities. The observer actualizes one of the existing potentialities and becomes part of the history of the atomic event. Since more than one alternative is open, there is room for novelty in nature and its history can be viewed as unique and unrepeatable. It has been argued that atomic indeterminacy allows room for God's providential activity through his control of naturally determined probabilities.[31] If such a view does not limit God's action to the atomic level only, it can be a useful way to correlate divine sovereignty with natural law.

The holistic Christian view parallels the emerging scientific idea that all events are related to their environment at various levels of organization and activity. This relational view sees nature in terms of interpenetrating fields and integrated systems rather than isolated and independent particles. Every entity is constituted by its relationships and participation within a larger system and thus is more than the sum of its parts. The interrelatedness of the parts interacting to form a given whole establishes new properties which are not deducible from the parts even though dependent on them.[32] Since different levels of organization and activity involve distinctive relationships and processes, they cannot be reduced to a single level of explanation.

Relational concepts can be correlated with the biblical view of the person as a unity of mind and body, related to God, nature and other persons. Mental events involve higher levels of activity in an integrated system. New patterns of organization produce alternative potentialities at various levels, allowing for choice and freedom at the higher levels.

Extending this approach to the social level suggests a parallel with the biblical ideal of interdependence and mutual service rather than the mechanistic concept of autonomous individualism. From this perspective persons can be seen as relational and responsible beings. Their uniqueness lies especially in their capacity for a relationship with God through Christ. The male-female relation distinctively images the triune relation in God.[33] This relational view allows for both physical and personal qualities in a complex unity of fact and value amenable to both science and theology. It has begun to emerge in the practice of science in such fields as holistic medicine and ecology with its emphasis on environmental relations and interdependence, and opens new perspectives for Christian concern.

Perspectives on a Christian View of Nature
The Christian view of multiple relationships between God, nature and persons calls for special responsibilities and ethical considerations. Since God values nature independently of its benefits to us, we are obligated to protect and preserve it. Science can aid in this conserving process, but too often the activities and results of science lead to exploitation of the earth's resources, irresponsible destruction of life and pollution of the environment. An *ethic of joy* in the goodness and beauty of nature as a gift of God will guard against these perversions, seeking to celebrate and uphold the value

of all the varied forms of life and creation (Ps 95). It will take greater care in such potentially dangerous developments as pesticides, genetic manipulations and radioactive materials.

The biblical view of evil helps to avoid the naive attitude that assumes complete autonomy for science. Awareness of sin carries with it the expectation of judgment on the use of illicit means or ends. Human fallibility and finite resources require the acceptance of limits. The demands of justice must take priority over the unlimited pursuit of knowledge, power or possessions. An *ethic of faith* in the moral order of nature and culture as revealed in Scripture will lead to the humility to accept God-given limits (Heb 11). It will provide the basis for preserving the balance of nature and ensuring the social justice and personal righteousness that can prevent human misery and world destruction.

The biblical mandate of stewardship is intended to fulfill God's purposes and to work against the effects of evil in the world. Responsibility and creativity are needed to realize the God-given potential for dominion within appropriate limits. The possibility of constructive change grows out of this tension between creative stewardship and limiting constraints. An *ethic of hope* will motivate this kind of responsible human creativity (Rom 8). It will guide the actions and applications of science, avoiding the judgment reserved for those who bury the wealth entrusted to them.

Finally, the biblical ideal of community is reflected in the developing awareness of the organic wholeness of nature and interdependence of humanity (1 Cor 12). It provides a worthy model for human relationships. An *ethic of love* is the basis for community and the source of real justice (1 Cor 13). It is the best solution to the problem of equitable distribution of limited resources. It ensures the just use of techniques, avoiding the dehumanizing results of specialization and division of labor. It allows for the richness of variety within the wholeness of unity.

A Christian view of the physical world is magnificently summarized by the psalmist from a creation perspective. First is a vision of God's glory displayed in the universe:

O LORD, our Lord,

How majestic is Thy name in all the earth,
Who hast displayed Thy splendor above the heavens!
From the mouth of infants and nursing babes
 Thou hast established strength,
Because of Thine adversaries,
To make the enemy and the revengeful cease. (Ps 8:1-2 NASB)

The world is seen as good and beautiful, a place to be observed and admired as a revelation of God. The reference to infants is reflected in the Incarnation with its vindication of the value of the material world and its promise of redemption from evil and its effects. The validity of experimental science with its activities of creative appreciation through devoted study of nature are thus reaffirmed.

Next is a revelation of God's power and wisdom, and his concern and goodness toward humanity:

When I consider Thy heavens, the work of Thy fingers,
The moon and the stars, which Thou hast ordained;
What is man, that Thou dost take thought of him?
And the son of man, that Thou dost care for him?
Yet Thou hast made him a little lower than God,
And dost crown him with glory and majesty! (Ps 8:3-5 NASB)

The order and intelligibility of the universe is here compared with human dependence and dignity. Our uniqueness as persons created in the image of God confirms that we transcend nature and have the creative and rational powers to consider and comprehend the creation. This affirms the basis for theoretical science as well as the capacity for critical evaluation of theories and their significance for a Christian world view.

Lastly is a reaffirmation of the creation mandate and the responsibility delegated to humanity for creation:

Thou dost make him to rule over the works of Thy hands;
Thou hast put all things under his feet,
All sheep and oxen,
And also the beasts of the field,
The birds of the heavens, and the fish of the sea,
Whatever passes through the paths of the seas.
O LORD, our Lord,

How majestic is Thy name in all the earth! (Ps 8:6-9 NASB) The task of responsible stewardship in exercising dominion gives purpose and meaning to historical existence. It also provides motivation and guidance for applied science and the kind of constructive participation that will preserve human values and protect the natural environment, recognizing it as a gift from God.

Thus a Christian view of the physical world sees nature in the light of Scripture and with a concern for culture. This involves a creative view of nature that recognizes the world as real and good. It includes a critical view of scientific ideas and methods that looks to Scripture for guidance, and for faith in the order and intelligibility revealed in creation. And it attempts a constructive view of culture that finds purpose and meaning in seeking to improve the world for the good of humanity and the glory of God.

4
Furthering
the Kingdom
in Psychology

Kirk E. Farnsworth

You're not free: it's your grandfather's itch you're scratching.
You have no dignity: you're not a man,
you're a rat in a vat of rewards and punishments,
you think you've chosen the rewards, you haven't:
the rewards have chosen you.[1]

The poet laments the loss of his freedom, his dignity and his
creativity. Modern psychology has taken it all away. Or at least
that's what he seems to think. Psychologist B. F. Skinner even goes
so far as to say that writing a poem is actually "having" a poem,
much as a mother "has" a baby or a hen lays an egg—and they all
feel better afterward.[2] A poet does not create a poem, according to
Skinner. It is merely the product of his or her genetic makeup and
environmental history.

What about freedom, dignity and creativity? Is Skinner's conclusion compatible with a Christian view of personhood? How can we
tell? If we decide the answer is no, then does that mean everything
else Skinner says is unchristian? And as the momentum builds, do
we conclude that all of psychology is unbiblical, and ultimately that
it is "of the devil"?

I would hope that today's college students are more astute than
that. In fact, I know they generally are. Therefore, I can limit my

task to the question, "How can we tell?" How can we tell or discern if what we are learning from psychology is what God wants us to regard as truth? Are there some guidelines for accepting others' psychological conclusions, as well as arriving at our own psychological conclusions and applying them to our lives with the confidence that they are helping us to further the kingdom of God?

Our job is to learn to think Christianly about psychology. This will involve another limiting of the task at hand: I will not be outlining a Christian psychology as a distinct body of knowledge. My goal will be to establish some minimal guidelines for Christian discernment in the three main areas of psychological activity: theory, research and practice.

World View

"Guidelines for thinking" is one way to think of a world view. Basically, a world view is the collection of underlying presuppositions from which one's thoughts and actions stem. A Christian world view is comprised of those fundamental Christian beliefs that most adequately describe the God-creation distinction and relationship.[3]

I need to clarify, briefly, my use of the term *world view*, with a somewhat expanded version of the basic definition. First, I conceive of a world view as a *conceptual framework*, not as a comprehensive accumulation of doctrines. It is just the most fundamental beliefs about God and his creation that can provide some limits and suggest some priorities for psychological thinking within a Christian framework. It is not a composite of all the doctrines of the church that answers every question psychology can ask and even some that it does not ask.

Second, a world view is *preconceptual* as well as conceptual. I believe that, in addition to cognition, personality is an important factor in thinking Christianly about psychology. By *preconceptual* I mean before thought, and feeling-oriented. For example, my felt-sense of beauty, as an unspoken expression of my deeply felt appreciation of God's creation, might in and of itself lead me to accept one psychological conclusion over another. According to Walter Thorson, referring to the work of Michael Polanyi, "unmistakably it is a sense of beauty which moves us to prefer some theories to others, and even to heuristically commit ourselves to them even though as yet we have no clear conception of their consequences."[4]

Third, I wish to emphasize the *process* of world-view thinking as much as the product. I prefer to focus on the dynamic nature of doing Christian thinking as well as on the more static nature of having Christian thoughts. The emphasis, then, is on using as well as having a Christian world view and on the struggle to discover truth at least as much as the security of possessing truth.

Components. The components of a world view can be referred to as *control beliefs*. For the Christian, these are the fundamental beliefs about the God-creation distinction and relationship that one arrives at out of one's Christian commitment. Such beliefs are not necessarily drawn exclusively from the Bible and some tend to be quite general.[5] The more general control beliefs, those that undergird other more specialized control beliefs, are the biblical doctrines of creation, sin, redemption and hope. They are foundational to every Christian's faith.

Nicholas Wolterstorff claims that since every scientist depends in part on control beliefs anyway (such as the necessity of measurement), Christians should depend on theirs in the same manner.[6] This means utilizing them both in the conduct of research and in discerning the value of the results of research. Arthur Holmes also recommends that Christians ferret out the influence of non-Christian assumptions and bring their Christian control beliefs to bear in their place.[7] And Stephen Evans reminds us that our fundamental beliefs must be kept in balance.[8] Thus, as we do research and decide on the value of research results, and as we replace non-Christian assumptions with Christian ones, we must keep in mind God's continuous acts of creation right along with our willful rebellion against our Creator (Upholder) and our redemption through his grace.

By utilizing our control beliefs as we interact with psychology, and by keeping them in balance, we can certainly go a long way in discerning with confidence what we can take from psychology to help to further the kingdom of God. For example, the doctrine of creation reminds us of our *creatureliness* and the accompanying reassurance that while we are not gods we are not garbage either. This is the basis for both our confidence in our self-worth and our refusal to engage in self-worship. Thus, I get an almost automatically negative, gut-level reaction to such "pop-psych" book titles as *I Ain't Much, Baby—But I'm All I've Got, Looking Out for Number One* and *How to Be Your Own Best Friend!*

Awareness of our creatureliness is also the basis for our humility in deciding how to react to comparative psychological research with nonhuman animals. Although humans make responsible choices and take purposeful actions, we can learn about some of the limits to our freedom by studying animals that are lower in the order of creation but not totally different from humans.

As we keep our control beliefs in balance, we can also see that a psychological theory of personality, education or psychotherapy that ignores our creatureliness and accepts a "horticultural view" of the self must be rejected. A horticultural view assumes a person is filled with goodness that just needs to be allowed to ooze out, like a rose unfolding from a rosebud, unencumbered by any sort of structure or limitation; it assumes no sin. Further, through our awareness of both sin and redemption we can enthusiastically avoid any psychological theory or practice that is thoroughly infused with pessimism toward the future, that assumes no divine intervention in an individual's life.

In addition to the general foundational control beliefs listed above, a Christian world view needs to include some more specialized control beliefs in order to function effectively in critiquing a discipline. Such beliefs will help us be more explicit in thinking Christianly about psychological theory, research and practice. We will perhaps not find the same extent of agreement as with the four general foundational beliefs, however. Consequently, when we decide on what specialized control beliefs to bring together to round out our Christian world view, we may find that our Christian world view differs from someone else's Christian world view. There is considerable room for variation. With this in mind, I will suggest three specialized control beliefs which I think are crucial in bringing a Christian perspective to psychology. They are beliefs concerning relationships, humanness and servanthood, and they are associated with theory, research and practice, respectively.

Relationship. We are relational beings. As John Donne has so vividly put it:

> No man is an island, entire of itself; every man is a piece of the continent, a part of the main. If a clod be washed away by the sea, Europe is the less, as well as if a promontory were, as well as if a manor of thy friend's or of thine own were: any man's death diminishes me, because I am involved in mankind, and therefore never send to know for whom the bell tolls; it tolls for thee.[9]

Because of our creatureliness, we are dependent—on God, on others, on nature. It is the kind of relatedness that is best expressed by the Hebrew dream of *shālōm:* "The harmony of a caring community informed at every point by its awareness of God."[10] Bishop John Taylor delineates the dream for us:

> The blessedness of this inter-related, God-related community might be thought of either as wholeness or as harmony. The wholeness was the all-inclusiveness of the framework of reference; the harmony was the reciprocity of all the parts. It meant a dancing kind of inter-relationship, seeking something more free than equality, more generous than equity, the ever-shifting equipoise of a life-system.[11]

So as relational beings we are dependent on God, others and nature for our sustenance, and we are answerable to God to fit our own needs to the needs of others and the surrounding environment.

Humanness. Human beings are unified beings who act as well as react. This implies wholeness and responsibility. According to Evans, the primary biblical emphasis regarding human beings is on wholeness:

> Humans possess an essential unity. They are not to be conceived as a series of isolated or disconnected events but as self-shaping beings who bear the consequences of previous choices and strive to achieve future ideals. . . . [This is] the concept of the self

as a unified whole. This unified wholeness is pre-eminent.[12]

Concerning the responsibility aspect of our humanness, Holmes states:

> If the relational character of the human person is one dominant theme that confronts us in Scripture, a second and equally dominant theme is that God holds us responsible. This fact of being obligated and answerable to God is overwhelmingly clear, and distinguishes humans from other earthlings.[13]

As human beings, then, we are unified beings who are not reducible to less than whole persons, and who are responsible before God for our ability, although limited, to transcend environmental determinants and make self-determining choices.

Servanthood. Christians are called to actively serve others. This is a high calling, for God cares for and is committed to his servants. We see this clearly in the servanthood of the entire nation of Israel:

> Listen to me, O my servant Israel, O my chosen ones: The Lord who made you, who will help you, says, O servant of mine, don't be afraid. O Jerusalem, my chosen ones, don't be afraid. For I will give you abundant water for your thirst and for your parched fields. And I will pour out my Spirit and my blessings on your children. (Is 44:1-3 LB)

The clearest picture of what a servant actually does is at the individual level, in the person of Jesus Christ. Again, Isaiah gives us that picture:

> See my servant, whom I uphold; my Chosen One, in whom I delight. I have put my Spirit upon him; he will reveal justice to the nations of the world. He will be gentle—he will not shout nor quarrel in the streets. He will not break the bruised reed, nor quench the dimly burning flame. He will encourage the faint-hearted, those tempted to despair. He will see full justice given to all who have been wronged. (Is 42:1-3 LB)

So with Jesus as our guide, it is evident that servanthood involves being gentle and not quarrelsome, bearing with the weak and infirm, building up those who are discouraged and bringing justice to those who have been wronged.

In other words, servanthood involves submission, sacrifice and service. These are the qualities of life that we are called to as followers of Jesus. Jesus himself came not to be served but to serve, and he expects us to do the same as good and faithful servants.

Theory

The first area of psychological endeavor that I will look at from a Christian perspective is theory. The control belief that I have chosen to associate with psychological theory is the Christian belief concerning relationship. The fundamental belief that we are relational beings seems directly counter to what is happening in much of psychological theorizing, particularly in the "self" theories of personality. Many theorists such as Erich Fromm, Abraham Maslow, Carl Rogers and Lawrence Kohlberg, and the self-helpers who utilize their theories, focus almost exclusively on the fulfillment of the individual outside of the context of relationship with others. This sort of blatant individualism, or selfism, is getting a lot of attention these days from Christians and non-Christians alike.

Individualism. "From 'Anities and 'Alities and 'Ologies and 'Isms, Good Lord, deliver us."[14] Individualism is certainly one of those "isms" from which we need to be delivered. The preoccupation with "me" has become a "growth industry" and has permeated much of our psychological knowledge about people. It needs to be challenged. One of the most recent books to do so, *Psychology's Sanction for Selfishness* by Michael and Lise Wallach, claims that the theories of most of the psychologists in this century have eroded three of the major areas of meaning in people's lives: work, marriage and children.[15]

Wallach and Wallach believe that the erosion is so all-encompassing because almost all psychologists share a particular assumption about motivation: people are not genuinely motivated by concern for the welfare of others. They are, rather, motivated by the satisfaction of their own needs and desires. There are differences in expressing the consensus, but nevertheless most theorists are in basic agreement. Wallach and Wallach go on to say:

We can find a Fromm or a Rogers or a Maslow believing we

should trust self-expression because human nature, left to its own devices, is essentially wholesome. Troubles are viewed as coming from the outside society, whose constraints and coercions oppress us. The task therefore is to find a mode of living that is truly expressive of, and really satisfying to, the individual in question. Let the person's nature rise up and manifest itself; it is to be trusted. But we can also find a Freud arguing that too much attempted goodness goes against our less-than-wholesome nature and therefore bespeaks neurosis. Therapy must act to relieve the pangs of conscience that otherwise are marshaled against the pleasures we seek for ourselves; it must free us to pursue our satisfactions with more impunity. Thus, hardly an optimist about human nature, Freud ends up at a similar place: the necessity of expressing and gratifying ourselves.[16]

According to Wallach and Wallach, different approaches all arrive at the same point of blaming society for inhibiting human nature, for keeping it in bondage. The aim of their therapies, then, is to promote greater self-acceptance and self-fulfillment, and to condemn society's pressures and the expectations of others for our troubles.

The Wallachs' critique suggests that we are being mystified into thinking that others are to blame for our troubles, so the way to avoid trouble in the future is to seek self-fulfillment and avoid commitment to others and their expectations. The point is well taken, but I have to disagree that all theorists and therapists see things from such a selfish perspective.

Another very recent book, *Psychological Seduction* by William Kilpatrick, complains that self-absorption is the "good news" of the psychological "gospel." But as it turns out, it is really bad news:

We are forced to entertain the possibility that psychology and related professions are proposing to solve problems that they themselves have helped to create. We find psychologists raising people's expectations for happiness in this life to an inordinate level, and then we find them dispensing advice about the mid-life crisis and dying. We find psychologists making a virtue out of self-preoccupation, and then we find them surprised at the increased supply of narcissists. We find psychologists advising the courts that there is no such thing as a bad boy or even a bad adult, and then we find them formulating theories to explain the rise in crime. We find psychologists severing the bonds of family life, and then we find them conducting therapy for broken families.[17]

Again, the point is a good one, but I do not think the case against psychology is as strong as Kilpatrick thinks it is. We should use the correlations that he mentions as suggestive for possible correction, not as proof of causation. In other words, if psychologists are in fact involving themselves more in the divorce than in the reconciliation of married couples, and if they are also conducting therapy with an ever-increasing number of broken families, then we should show concern that one is not feeding off the other. It does not necessarily mean, however, that one is causing the other.

The comments that I have made so far about the promotion of individualism by psychology were drawn primarily from a clinical context. Wallach and Wallach, however, document the fact that similar comments apply to academic psychology. This is the context that affects students most directly, and the psychology textbook is the primary means for communicating to them the important information in psychology. The problem is that when textbooks present the conclusion about human motivation mentioned above, however tentatively it may be put forth,

> the qualifications tend to get lost, and what remain are presumptive formulations about human nature invested with an aura of scientific necessity. What the students carry away with them are, in their view, scientific laws or necessary truths about how we act. These tend to be taken . . . to have universality of application and broad generality, rather than reflecting some of what may go on in a particular culture at a given time with particular values such as individualism.[18]

One of the most influential theories in academic psychology today is social learning theory. Closely linked to the work of Albert Bandura, "social learning theory again makes the root assumption that all an individual can fundamentally care about are personal outcomes."[19] For example, the reason you are likely to be upset when a friend is in pain is not because you are empathetically sharing the burden but because, as pointed out by the Wallachs, you are afraid you might be hurt also.

Bandura even argues that something as innocent as playing a tuba solo is not done because it is satisfying in its own right, but only because of the anticipated approval of others.[20] And the reason that we take in certain standards and make them a basis for the self-regulation of our behavior is to gain social approval and to avoid social disapproval. This would be the reason for following biblical standards, according to Bandura. However, the absolute role that social learning theory ascribes to personal gain is, according to Wallach and Wallach, more of an article of faith than a compelling conclusion from experimental evidence.

Lawrence Kohlberg. Another influential theory in academic psychology is Lawrence Kohlberg's theory of moral development. Originally, it was comprised of three general levels and six specific stages describing the development of moral reasoning. The process begins at Level I, the "preconventional" level, where rules and social expectations are imposed by rewards and punishments. Moral judgment is in response to power figures. Level II, the "conventional" level, involves conformity to and identification with those rules and expectations that had been imposed from without. Here moral judgment is in anticipation of social praise and blame and is a response of personal loyalty. At Level III, the "postconventional" level, the person shakes loose from the external authority of accepted social standards and bases moral reasoning on self-chosen principles. Moral judgment, then, is in response to autonomous principles.

Within each level are two distinct stages. Stage 1 (Level I) is dominated by the physical consequences of behavior: the child simply defers to the superior position and power of the parent. In Stage 2 (Level I) deference is based on the benefit it will bring in return. Stage 3 (Level II) involves seeking the approval of others: to conform is to be good. Indeed, this stage is referred to as the "good boy-nice girl orientation." Stage 4 (Level II) originally emphasized maintenance of the social order of one's own group with a "law-and-order orientation." Recently, this emphasis has been expanded to include concern for society as a whole. Stage 5 (Level III) ushers in an entirely new ball game. Moral reasoning is no longer connected with one's specific reference group or groups, but operates freely within the general confines of individual rights as agreed upon by the larger society. Any situation that falls outside those confines becomes a matter of personal value or opinion. Finally, Stage 6 (Level III) arrives on the scene with moral reasoning based on self-chosen ethical principles. These principles are highly abstract, like the principle of human rights. They are not concrete moral rules, such as the Ten Commandments.

Stage 6, however, is now being phased out. That would be no great loss, since through the years it has been heavily criticized as elitist and antithetical to the building of community. Empirically, the idea has not held up: longitudinal studies have failed to turn up people who have achieved Stage 6. Consequently, "Kohlberg lamented at a recent symposium: 'Perhaps all the Sixth Stage persons of the 1960s had been wiped out, perhaps they had regressed, or maybe it was all my imagination in the first place.' "[21]

Kohlberg's latest interest has been in counteracting the growing privatism that he sees in today's youth. His goal is to help people attain Stage 4 in the sense of being good community members and good citizens. This sounds like he is becoming more compatible with the fundamental Christian belief that human beings are relational beings. But we had better be careful.

A Critique of the Theory of Moral Development. Nicholas Wolterstorff points out that Kohlberg is concerned only with form, to the total exclusion of content or substance.[22] His entire focus is on how someone reasons, not on what he or she reasons about. So the theory is more about cognitive development than it is about moral development. People actually develop from one level of cognitive ability to another—from one, it is assumed, universal pattern of reasoning to another.

This rather ominously suggests that, according to Kohlberg, morality is based on universal principles that are derived from individual reasoning alone. What it means is that a normative community—a community that supplies a standard for its members' morality—makes little if any contribution to the individual's discernment of moral principles. Kohlberg's heavy emphasis on the autonomy of the individual, who is neither dependent on nor answerable to the community, therefore makes his new-found interest in building community all form and no substance, just like his theory of moral development. This is surely not the emphasis on relationship that is fundamental to the Christian faith.

The proper context for the moral development of a Christian is not autonomy of the individual but relationship with the community. Specifically, it is dependence on and answerability to other believers.

> It is here that the structures of accountability, discipline and encouragement, confrontation and support will facilitate growth to the fullness of the stature of Jesus Christ. The meaning of moral terms emerges from the common object of worship. The reasons one gives for actions will be consonant with the vision of this community and not necessarily the larger human community. If the life of the Christian is a function of the encounter with the God who acts in history, then moral identity is dependent on the story of a particular people who recount Yahweh's dealing with them. The history of experiences of the Christian community becomes the history of the individual. The Christian life is narrative dependent.[23]

William Kilpatrick also picks up the narrative theme. He notes that with Kohlberg's approach "there is no suggestion that right and wrong can actually be known, no training in virtues, no models to imitate, and finally, no stories."[24] In order to have character, he continues, one must be a "character in a story," not a "character at large" bound only to one's own development. Kilpatrick concludes:

> It is not enough to comprehend a moral situation, you must also care about it; and it is one of the peculiarities of [Kohlberg's] approach that it lacks any power to make us care. [His technique of discussing moral dilemmas reveals] characters in the dilemmas [that] are cardboard cutouts. We have no interest in them,

only in their case. The dilemmas are stories of a kind, but they are dehydrated stories. There is no juice in them. One cannot imagine parents passing down to their children the "Saga of the Starving Wife and the Stolen Food." A dilemma—still less a neutral values discussion—provides no model of virtue for us to follow. A young person might very well be able to derive some valid moral principles from discussions of these cases, but a principle is a good deal less than half the moral equation.[25]

In summary, individualism is a major problem with several psychological theories. A Christian world view, that includes the fundamental belief that humans are relational beings, calls into question those theories that promote the development and fulfillment of the individual outside the context of relationship with others. Among the assumptions that must be challenged are that self-fulfillment is better than concern for the welfare of others, self-absorption is a virtue, self-gain is all that matters, and self-autonomy is preferable to dependence on and answerability to a reference group.

Research

Research is the second area of psychological activity that I will look at from a Christian perspective. The control belief that is most readily associated with psychological research is humanness. This is the fundamental belief that human beings are unified beings, irreducible to parts or disconnected processes and able to make self-determining choices for which they are responsible as persons.

According to Stephen Evans, however, "it is fair to say that the rise of the human sciences in the twentieth century has been marked by the demise of the person. That is, there is a definite tendency to avoid explanations of human behavior which appeal to the conscious decisions of persons in favor of almost any nonpersonal factors."[26] Some of the reason for that can undoubtedly be attributed to the dehumanizing presuppositions that many psychologists carry with them into their research.

Presuppositions can be spoken of as "isms." I have already discussed individualism in connection with psychological theory, and would add several to the list that affect psychological research. They include reductionism (the whole is nothing but what is represented by a smaller part or the sum of all the parts—man is nothing but . . .), determinism (behavior always has a prior cause—freedom is an illusion) and materialism (the universe is composed of only matter and energy—internal mental states, although they occur, do not cause behavior but are merely epiphenomenal). These three are obviously contrary to the control belief of humanness as described above.

In addition, I would include two presuppositions that are not as directly opposed to humanness as I have defined it, but that are most definitely incompatible with it. They are evolutionism and behaviorism. Let us examine these two a bit further.

Evolutionism. Evolutionism begins with the assumption that humans evolved from lower animals. It then goes beyond ordinary comparative psychological research that is based on the observed similarities across species of anatomical structures and physiological functions, and further assumes that behavioral processes are also alike. This presupposition can also be referred to as *ratomorphism.*

Ratomorphism is a clever name for arguing through analogy with animals. In other words, the same label is attached to human and, let us say, rat behaviors that look similar. And if the rat behaviors are thoroughly understood, then it is claimed that the human behaviors can be explained in the same way. The problem is that, although the analogies sound plausible, they have only their plausibility for support.

The flip side of ratomorphism is really interesting. Here the analogy is reversed so that human qualities can be attributed to animals. For example, Harry Harlow has induced "psychopathology" in rhesus monkeys by isolating them until they become "depressed."[27] During prolonged periods of separation from their mothers, young monkeys were observed to cease playing together and to become withdrawn and inactive. This was termed "depressive behavior" or "depressive withdrawal."

In another study, Harlow rigged up a vertical chamber apparatus. "Depression in humans has been characterized as a state of 'helplessness and hopelessness, sunken in a well of despair,' and the chambers were designed to reproduce such a well for monkey subjects."[28] The result of confinement in the chambers for even a relatively short period of time was "profound and prolonged depression" in the monkeys.

I seriously question Harlow's conclusions. Is "monkey depression" really the same as a human person's experience of what it is like to be depressed? Is the desolate human experience referred to as "a well of despair" at all comparable to what it is like for a monkey to be confined, literally, in a well? And, from the perspective of a Christian world view, are these conclusions and the degree of continuity between humans and lower forms of animal life that they represent at all reconcilable with fundamental belief in the undiminished humanness of the human being?[29]

Behaviorism. According to behaviorism, a person is conditioned by the environment to respond in various ways that can be measured. Philosophically, behaviorism is committed to the belief that humans are infinitely malleable. Thus, all problems are seen as social problems that will disappear when the social environment is properly manipulated. This is the quintessence of B. F. Skinner's social vision.

Technologically, behaviorism is committed to the identifying characteristics of the natural sciences, such as laboratories, impersonal procedures and measurement. An example of this commitment can be seen in the present status of cognitive psychology, the currently fashionable approach to the study of how people perceive, remember and think. Ulric Neisser, the acknowledged father of cognitive psychology, is not happy with how the distinctive features of the natural sciences have taken control of his "baby":

> Most experimental cognitive psychology has taken a narrowly academic view of human abilities. The subjects of most experiments are given very artificial test-like tasks. They might be asked to repeat how many dots appeared, or classify characters, or say whether two forms are identical or not. They are *not* supposed to get bored, wonder whether the experiment is worth doing, respond for their own amusement, or quit. Yet often these would be intelligent courses of action. . . .

The prevailing view in [cognitive] psychology is usually one that is most convenient for us and least convenient for the people we theorize about. Psychologists rubricize people—put them into categories. They reduce mental processes to the simplest possible terms. They say, it's all association, or it's all conditioning, or it's all X, where X is whatever the current psychological fashion dictates. Whatever X may be, and whatever good experiments may originally have determined X, it does serious injustice to any person who is thinking and acting and moving and feeling in the real world. . . . You've got to listen to how people say it is.[30]

A Christian critique would have to agree that an approach that rubricizes people and does not treat them as self-determining, responsible persons leaves a lot to be desired. The criteria for humanness are not being met, and yet behaviorism is in full bloom. Everything is explained by the word "conditioning," subjects are given artificial tasks not found in the real world (like counting dots), and people are not listened to.

Neisser highlights the fact that psychological research can be good but not relevant. It can be rigorous but not significant. This has been a strength and a weakness of behavioristic psychology: the well-designed experiment with unintended consequences.

Chris Argyris has discovered some of the unintended consequences of highly rigorous research. He has also found the properties of well-designed research to be remarkably similar to the properties of—of all things—formal organizations: "Rigorousness is to a researcher what efficiency is to an executive. . . . Moreover, many of the dysfunctions reported between experimenter and subject are similar to the dysfunctions between management and employee."[31]

Argyris made his comparisons by initially summarizing the criteria for conducting rigorous research. First is the removal of ambiguity from the problem being investigated and the relevant variables. The emphasis is on ease of observing variables and measuring them. Second is maximum control by the researcher over those variables. He then found that the criteria create conditions for the subject (where behavior is tightly defined, controlled and evaluated) that are very similar to (in Argyris's words) the most mechanized assembly-line conditions.

Argyris was then able to observe that, because of the close similarity between the conditions in organizations and the conditions in rigorous research, the same unintended consequences caused by the former can be connected to the latter. They include, in the language of research, such things as "psychological withdrawal while remaining physically in the research situation, . . . knowingly giving incorrect answers, being a difficult subject, second-guessing the research design and trying to circumvent it in some fashion, producing the minimally accepted amount of behavior, coercing others to produce minimally, and disbelief and mistrust of the researcher."[32]

Deception. Argyris highlights, among other things, the fact that psychological research can cause mistrust. Probably one of the biggest factors contributing to such a negative consequence is the widespread practice of deception. For years the professional orthodoxy has been the assumption that first-person information is not as valid as third-person information. People in general are not capable of giving accurate, unbiased accounts of their experience. They do not know themselves well enough to be accurate and are too defensive to be unbiased. Since "self report" cannot be relied upon, people must be deceived in order to discover their real thoughts.

As extreme as these assumptions might seem, deception became standard operating procedure during the 1960s. Zick Rubin reports that:

> To study social behavior "scientifically," researchers created trumped-up situations and then observed their subjects' reactions. To explore the impact of self-esteem on behavior, for example, researchers gave subjects glowing or damning "reports" on their maturity. To investigate the effects of guilt, they told subjects that they had broken a piece of equipment.[33]

Such trickery is still flourishing today. "Stooges" are posing as fellow subjects but secretly following prearranged scripts; subjects are being given false reports about "test" results, and on and on it goes. Deception, according to Rubin, is just being taken for granted. It is alarming to many Christians and non-Christians alike that such underhanded procedures are so common, at least in some areas of psychology.

With the help of a Christian world view, however, we can rise above the mentality that by learning how to do deceptive research we can thereby learn how to know people better than they can know themselves and report that knowledge. Christian students, for example, who are being taught detached, devious research procedures can balance the effects of such teaching with the control belief that persons act as well as react, making self-determining choices as responsible beings. With that in mind, students can begin to learn what psychology has to say about dialog rather than detachment and trust rather than deception. They can learn how to build trusting relationships so others can know themselves as truthfully as possible and communicate that understanding as accurately as possible.

Salt or City. There are many things related to research that students can learn, in addition to building trusting relationships, that are good psychology as well as compatible with a Christian world view. Some have to do with biblically oriented research priorities, some with person-centered research methods and some with the ethical application of research results. The resulting "Christian psychology" can function as either "salt of the earth" or a "city on a hill." It can make its presence felt in the profession of psychology either through interaction as a corrective or through separation as an alternative.

We can find examples of both the salt and city metaphors in the literature. For example, two Christian psychologists have written recently about changes in psychology from a Christian perspective that would serve as a constructive alternative—as a city on a hill— to mainline psychology.[34] Several other Christian psychologists have written about using Christian principles as correctives in constructive interaction—as salt—with mainline psychology.

One has done a Christian world-view critique of the work of B. F. Skinner, with the result being acceptance of many of his scientific contributions as differentiated from his speculative ones. Another has pointed out, from a Christian standpoint, some of the values as well as dangers of studying animal behavior to learn more about human behavior. Another has written four books on the complementary nature of psychology and theology, with the purpose of showing how Christian control beliefs interact positively with a wide variety of psychological research findings.[35]

Practice

The third common area of psychological activity is practice. One of the most popular types of psychological practice, especially among Christians, is counseling. What would a Christian perspective emphasize, then, in an area of such growing importance within the church today?

I would strongly recommend that Christian students bring to their consideration of counseling as a career an emphasis on the fundamental belief that Christians are called to serve others. This is the control belief of servanthood. Counseling is a ministry of servanthood and as such involves service to others and sacrifice for the welfare of others.

One would be well advised, however, to note how easy it is to forget about being a servant when one is caught up in being or becoming a professional counselor. Even "Christian counseling" can shift away from the distinctiveness of being a church-sponsored service ministry to full participation in the secularized, professionally sanctioned service *industry*. It is imperative for the Christian desiring to go into the helping professions to resist the gradual but powerful entrapment of secular professionalism.

Professionalism. One way to describe psychological counseling when it loses its servant mentality and becomes part of a service industry governed by secular professionalism is that it takes on some of the characteristics of a business. As a business, counseling needs clients. One sure way to get them is to come up with a unique technique and then define some need that can be remedied only by that technique. If the need and its remedy are marketed right, many people will have their needs defined for them and will become dependent on the new counseling technique for relief. It reminds me of a bunch of dermatologists proclaiming that baldness is a disease, because they are unemployed.

As a business, counseling also must operate in compliance with certain legal guidelines. These are not bad in and of themselves. They provide an ethical norm against which professional conduct can be evaluated as a guarantee for the consumer of counseling services. A problem arises, however, when the use of professional standards becomes a kind of legalism.

The Christian student should take note of how easy it is for a Christian in the professions to be a Christian person on the one hand and a professional person on the other. The two "persons" can be kept split apart, it is assumed, because it combines the best of both worlds: Christian morality and professional ethics. What could be better than to be served by a Christian who scrupulously abides by the ethics of his or her profession? This is the kind of splitting of worlds—the kind of legalism—I would suggest, that Aleksandr Solzhenitsyn had in mind when he delivered the commencement address at Harvard University a few years ago. At one point in his address he referred to the legalism issue specifically, when he described the "legalistic life":

> Every conflict is solved according to the letter of the law and this is considered to be the ultimate solution. If one is right from a legal point of view, nothing more is required, nobody may mention that one could still not be entirely right, and urge self-restraint or a renunciation of these rights, call for sacrifice and selfless risk: this would simply sound absurd. Voluntary self-restraint is almost unheard of: everybody strives toward further expansion to the extreme limit of the legal frames. . . .
>
> I have spent all my life under a Communist regime and I will tell you that a society without any objective legal scale is a terrible one indeed. But a society with no other scale but the legal one is also less than worthy of man. . . . Whenever the tissue of life is woven of legalistic relationships, this creates an atmosphere of spiritual mediocrity that paralyzes man's noblest impulses.[36]

Accountability to the ethics of one's profession as the upper limit of one's responsibility is what Solzhenitsyn was referring to. If the

profession will allow it, it must be okay: nothing more—or less—
is required. Self-restraint, personal sacrifice, selfless risk: they
sound absurd to the world and are unnecessary according to the
profession. This may be adequate for being a "good" professional,
but it is also the basis for the spiritual mediocrity of which Solzhenitsyn speaks.

The issue for the Christian counselor is one of ultimate accountability. It is an issue of lordship of one's professional life. Will it be
a legalistic life or one that is more—and less—than that, one that
is committed to the lordship of Jesus Christ at every point?

I have developed the full scope of the problem of professionalism
elsewhere.[37] What is of concern here is that Christian students
realize the tremendous impact they can have on the counseling
profession and on individual lives through a counseling ministry if
they consistently hold to a Christian world view. The counseling
profession needs servants who are committed more to service and
self-sacrifice than to making money and a name for themselves.

A Counseling Career. In considering counseling as a career, the
student should first think through as a Christian what a career is.
Most importantly, a counseling career is not a personal possession.
No career is, for the Christian. From a Christian perspective, one's
career emerges out of and is committed to seeking first the kingdom
of God (Mt 6:33). The focus is on the kingdom, not on the career.
Therefore, one's counseling career must be regarded as within the
realm of overall stewardship. The emphasis must be on giving, not
taking, on furthering the kingdom through service to others, not
advancing oneself by furthering one's career.[38]

A counseling career is also not a self-indulgent escalator of money
and status. Although one should cultivate one's professional field
with ethical self-discipline, it is inappropriate for the Christian
counselor to heavily plant it with economic self-interest. That
would be far removed from the selfless sacrifice referred to by
Solzhenitsyn, and it would certainly not be compatible with a
servanthood view of counseling.

Second, a Christian student should look carefully at a variety of
graduate counseling programs from the perspective of a Christian

world view. Which ones seem to emphasize serving people as much as getting credentials? Which ones seem to prepare students for personal sacrifice as well as for financial gain?

Looking at Christian graduate counseling programs presents the student with similar questions but more of them. You expect more from a program based on Christian principles, and you want to make sure you get it. Some programs may be Christian in name only, however. For instance, it is possible for a program to be thoroughly professional and fail to be uniquely Christian. That is winning the battle but losing the war. Certainly Christian counselors must be competent enough to possess the same credentials as anyone else, but that is only the battle for recognition. The real battle—the war—is for the redemption of persons and institutions by bringing them under the lordship of Jesus Christ. That is the spiritual war that some Christian counseling programs may need to begin to wage.

For example, some Christian counseling programs may need to apply Christian principles to their organizational administrative structure, structures for articulating personnel policies and for implementing procedures to carry them out, and academic structures for deciding the content of their course offerings. The outcome would hopefully be similar in kind to what the prophet Jeremiah (9:23-24, paraphrased) said long ago. Let them boast not in their wisdom (their students all scored very high on the entrance exams), in their might (their faculty have published countless books and articles in professional journals), or in their riches (their program is fully endowed). Rather, let them boast in administrative decision making and personnel policies based on *loving-kindness*, a curriculum that is permeated with a concern for *justice*, and an educational community where caring relationships among faculty, students, administration and staff foster *righteousness* in each other.

Finally, after putting the counseling profession and the educational context for counselor preparation into Christian perspective, the student should begin thinking about the context for his or her actual counseling practice. What would the best context be for bringing one's counseling activities under the lordship of Jesus

Christ? Probably the most generally applicable approach would be to establish a reference group of believers as the locus of one's professional accountability. Students would be well advised, then, to plan on making such a group central to their future counseling practice.

The function of a counselor's reference group is to act as a forum for prayerful discussion of and discernment concerning the compatibility of a Christian world view with such things as various counseling techniques, alternative fee structures and diverse staff relationships. The counselor is in turn accountable to the group to deal with any conflicts that may emerge. With the group's support and encouragement, counseling can truly be servanthood and Christ can truly be lord of one's counseling ministry. Christian students who are considering a career in counseling have much to look forward to.

We have now come full circle. The emphasis at the beginning of the chapter was on our dependence on and answerability to God, through Christian community. At the end of the chapter the emphasis is again on the centrality of a group of believers. This is the most suitable context for students who want to think and work constructively as Christians in the field of psychology. It is within this context that Christian students are encouraged to utilize a Christian world view to formulate their understanding of psychological theory, research and practice unencumbered by the distorting effects of individualism, evolutionism, behaviorism and professionalism. And it is within the context of believers that Christian students are empowered to enter the profession of psychology with a heightened awareness of their creaturehood, relatedness, humanness and servanthood—and with the high aim of building a better psychology and furthering the kingdom of God.

5
The
Creative
Arts

Leland Ryken

This is the final essay in a series that defines a Christian world view and applies that framework to leading areas of intellectual life. We must not allow the final position of this essay to mislead us into thinking that the creative arts are the extraneous "dessert" in a person's world view, an intellectual delicacy that cannot hope to compare in importance to such staples as philosophy and the physical and social sciences.

Creativity and imagination permeate all human activity. It is important to note at the outset, therefore, that the qualities that I attribute to the creative arts are present in other intellectual pursuits as well. My focus will be on the arts; I leave it to each reader to decide how widely my statements apply to the humanities in general and the social and natural sciences.

The Place of the Arts in a World View
The creative arts play a crucial role in shaping the world view of every person and culture. They are an implied declaration that a world view consists of more than abstract ideas or theoretical concepts. A world picture is a map of reality made up of images, symbols, myths and stories as well as theoretical concepts. Contemporary psychology has given us such terms as *preconceptual sensing* and

nonverbal cognition and the *right side of the brain* to identify what I will call images.

The arts are rooted in the image-making and image-perceiving nature of people. People do not live by ideas alone. They also express their affirmations and denials through the paint on a canvas, the tension and release of sound, and poems and stories. A noted theologian has said that "we are far more image-making and image-using creatures than we usually think ourselves to be and . . . are guided and formed by images in our minds. . . . Man . . . is a being who grasps and shapes reality . . . with the aid of great images, metaphors, and analogies."[1]

Who can doubt it? People organize their lives and make their decisions partly in terms of such images as heroes and villains, cross and altar, national emblem and patriotic legend, love song and hymn, landscape painting and portrait. These images have an ideational aspect to them but also communicate meanings that do not become focused into the form of theoretical propositions.[2]

By their very nature, therefore, the arts serve the salutary function of reminding people, including Christians, that to regard their world view as being solely the domain of theoretical thought is to invite unawareness about themselves. People may assent to the proposition that the true end of life is not to make money and accumulate possessions, but if their minds are filled with images of big houses and fancy clothes, their actual behavior will run in the direction of materialism. People may theoretically believe in the ideals of chastity and faithful wedded love, but if their minds are filled with images of exposed bodies and songs of seduction, their sexual behavior will have a large admixture of lust and sexual license in it.

Unless we recognize the powerful role of images in a world view, our world view and the behavior it produces will continue to be the muddled things they often are. We also need to recognize that the quality of our life and character is heavily affected by the quality of the images that we habitually take into our minds and imaginations.

The contribution that the arts make to a person's world view is rooted in the fact that they all employ a "language" of images. The visual artist, for example, uses physical materials such as paint and stone to produce images that we can see and touch. Music employs physical instruments to produce sounds that we hear with our ears and feel in our muscles. Poets use words to evoke imagined sensations, objects and emotions. And storytellers describe such tangible realities as people performing actions in physical settings.

The Imagination. The human faculty or capacity that enables the arts to image forth reality in this way is the imagination. Imagination is what the arts share. By "imagination" I mean simply the image-making and image-perceiving capacity that we all have; I do not have in mind any particular theory of artistic creativity or mental association. Modern aesthetic theory is based on the imagination as the key to everything, and it has stressed two aspects of the imagination.

Imagination implies, first of all, the notion of "image," that is, sensory concreteness or experiential immediacy. The arts are a *presentational* form. Instead of talking *about* human experience, they present the experience. The arts show rather than tell. They incarnate their meanings in concrete images of human experience or the external world. Instead of primarily asking our intellects to grasp an idea, the arts ask us to undergo an experience, which may or may not eventuate in a proposition or concept. The fiction writer Flannery O'Connor has said regarding her particular art form that "the whole story is the meaning, because it is an experience, not an abstraction."[3] We can view the arts as analogous to a picture accompanying the instructions for assembling an appliance or piece of furniture: if we have a good picture, we may not even need the written instructions.

The second thing that imagination implies is a fictional or imaginary element. Fictional literature is the most obvious illustration of the "made up" quality of art, but in fact all art is an imaginary reconstruction of actual reality. Looking at a painted landscape is never the same as standing in an actual landscape. Music gives us combinations of sounds that we never encounter in real life. Only in poems do people speak in rhyme and regular meter.

The arts are never a mere copy of life. They are always a distillation of some aspect of reality. All artists use techniques of highlighting, omission, selectivity, exaggeration, arrangement and juxtaposition to heighten our perception of some aspect of life. Music, for example, artificially produces arrangements of sounds that awaken feelings of serenity or exultation or reverence. A painting can give us a heightened sense of something as common as flowers and household utensils, as in the still-life paintings of the Dutch realists. Literary tragedy distills the essence of human suffering and silhouettes it with clarity.

The arts, in short, are based on a grand paradox. They are imaginary constructions that "distort" reality in order to increase our awareness of it. In the words of Pablo Picasso, "Art is a lie that makes us realize truth."[4] Or as Samuel Johnson put it, works of fiction "are not mistaken for realities, but . . . bring realities to mind."[5] The truth that the arts are particularly adept at capturing is enduring, elemental human experience. Whereas the newspaper and history book tell us what *happened,* the arts tell us what *happens*— the reality that never goes out of date because it is universal in human experience.

Imagination and the Bible. If we now ask how the artistic imagination fares in a Christian world view, it is at once apparent that Christianity affirms the artistic enterprise. The Bible itself endorses both the image-making and imaginary impulses of the arts. There are four main lines of evidence to support this claim.

The first is that God is portrayed in the Bible as a creator of images. A dominant theme throughout the Old Testament is God's creation of the natural world of created objects. These visible images, in turn, are said to communicate truth about God himself (Ps 19:1-4; Rom 1:19-20). The New Testament counterpart is the Incarnation of Jesus, who is declared to be God in tangible human form.

We should note secondly the literary nature of the Bible. The one thing that the Bible is *not* is what we so often picture it as being— a theological outline with proof texts attached. The bulk of the Bible consists of stories, poems, visions and letters, all of them literary forms. When asked to define *neighbor*, Jesus told a fictional story (Lk 10:25-37). When he wished to teach a lesson in servanthood, he washed his disciples' feet (Jn 13:1-20). Jesus taught religious truth by making up stories about sheep and pearls and seed and fish. Oliver Cromwell rightly said that Jesus "spoke *things*." Jesus trusted the ability of literary images to convey religious truth when he told his disciples to "remember Lot's wife" (Lk 17:32). The Bible repeatedly affirms the image-making tendency of the arts.

Third, the Christian sacraments of communion and baptism have also been important in attempts to arrive at a Christian aesthetic (philosophy of the arts). The Christian sacraments affirm the sign-making impulse of the arts. The sacraments, after all, use the physical elements of water, bread and wine to express and impart spiritual realities. While the Christian sacraments do not lend sanction to every manifestation of the creative imagination in a fallen world, they do nonetheless confirm the principle that images and symbols can express truth to the glory of God and the edification of people.

A fourth biblical validation of the arts is the descriptions of worship that we find especially in the Old Testament. Worship in the Bible is surrounded by a wealth of music and visual and verbal art.[6] As the Old Testament worshipers approached the Temple in Jerusalem, they saw two gigantic freestanding bronze pillars over twenty-five feet high (1 Kings 7:15-22). These monoliths had no architectural function other than to be beautiful and suggest by their aesthetic properties something of the grandeur, stability and power of God. The pillars were specimens of one prominent type of art in the Temple, namely, abstract or nonrepresentational art.

Representational and symbolic art were also present in Old Testament worship. The ten stands of bronze at the Temple were engraved with lions, oxen and palm trees (1 Kings 7:27-37). Sculptures of winged cherubim were prominent in both the tabernacle (Ex 25:18-20; 26:31) and the Temple (1 Kings 7:29). Symbolic art also abounded, with such tangible objects as a golden table for the sacred bread, a golden altar, lampstands of pure gold and basins serving as visual symbols of such spiritual realities as communion with God, sacrifice, revelation and cleansing.

There can be no doubt that the tabernacle and Temple were the Old Testament believer's most intense encounter with artistic beauty. If we doubt this, we need only read the chapters of the Bible that describe the visual properties of these places (Ex 25—31; 35—39; 1 Kings 5—7; 2 Chron 2—4). The descriptions testify to an overwhelming value accorded to beauty. Some of the artistic embellishment in these places of worship awakened the worshipers' awareness of the other great source of beauty in their life—nature, as seen, for example, in the carved flowers about which we read repeatedly (1 Kings 7).

The beauty associated with the tabernacle and Temple included the purely imaginary as well as the realistic. The pomegranates on Aaron's robe were colored blue, purple and scarlet. In nature there *are* no blue pomegranates. One of the most attractive artifacts at the Temple was a molten sea forty-five feet in circumference, filled with water and resting on twelve statuesque oxen (1 Kings 7:23-26). Where in the real world can one find a sea held up on the backs of oxen? Francis Schaeffer rightly comments that "Christian artists do not need to be threatened by fantasy and imagination. . . . The Christian is the one whose imagination should fly beyond the stars."[7]

Music was as prominent at the Temple as were the visual arts. David appointed four thousand musicians to conduct the music of the Temple (1 Chron 23:5). The Psalms, moreover, are a Temple hymnbook. If we catalog the musical instruments mentioned in the Psalms, they show the same wide use of available art forms that the visual arts in the Temple do.

It is no wonder that Christianity has been the most artistic religion in the world. Much of its doctrine has been enshrined in music, visual symbol, poem and story. The authoritative book of this revealed religion is itself a largely literary work in which story, character and image are the customary ways of embodying truth. For more than fifteen centuries of Western history, Christianity provided the main influence and content for the creative arts. That it lost its dominance is one of the tragedies of both Western civilization and Christendom. That the arts will someday regain their lost place among Christians is a thing to be hoped.

Perspective in the Arts

The main thesis of this entire book—that a person's world view affects all human pursuits —emphatically applies to the creation and study of the arts. The arts by their very nature are value-laden. They embody and express human values. Even the aspects of human experience that painters and composers and writers choose for artistic portrayal are an implied comment about what is important and worthy of attention.

And once they have selected their subject, artists express an attitude toward the subject. The arts are *affective:* they are constructed so as to encourage an audience to share the artist's way of experiencing or perceiving reality. Works of art by their nature awaken attitudes or feelings of sympathy and aversion, approval and disapproval toward the whole range of human experience.

While the importance of perspective in works of art is probably a truism, it is too often overlooked that the *study* of art, music and literature is just as influenced by perspective. Critics and teachers of the arts have a bias, too. They even reveal a bias in the works they choose to discuss or include in a course syllabus. And once they have chosen their works, they reveal a perspective in the aspects of a work that they single out for comment and in the attitudes they express toward the topics they have chosen for scrutiny. What critics and teachers of the arts *omit* from discussion can tell us as much about their bias as what they include. It would be a drastic mistake, therefore, to think that what a literature or art teacher says about works of art is any more "objective" than what a teacher of philosophy or biology says.

If art is inherently value-laden, so is the assimilation of art. As readers, viewers and listeners, we assimilate works of art within the framework of our personal experiences and world view. Experiencing and interpreting works of art are subjective activities. The final meaning of a painting or symphony or story is a fusion of what the work itself puts before a person and the content that a person is able to bring to the words on a page or the sounds from an instrument or the colors and objects on a canvas.

If experiencing art is this subjective, we are free as consumers of art to be ourselves when we read and listen and look. We do not need to repress our values or apologize for having a world view when we read a novel or visit an art gallery or attend a concert. We do, however, need to be self-aware about our responses. We should acknowledge the presuppositions that lead us to see certain elements in a work of art, and we need to extend the same charitable privilege to people who do not share those presuppositions and therefore respond differently.

Current aesthetic theory stresses the idea of "interpretive communities"—groups of people who view the creative arts from a common core of interests and assumptions and values. Christians are one such interpretive community. They are not inherently better artists or critics than other people are. But they have their own "agenda" of interests springing from their coherent world view. They also share beliefs and attitudes that they bring to their artistic and critical pursuits. The purpose of this essay is to delineate the Christian principles that have a special relevance to the arts.

As an organizing framework, we should note that artists perform three interrelated activities: (1) they create aesthetic objects and artistic form; (2) they present human experience for our contemplation; and (3) they offer an interpretation of the experiences they present. Perspective affects all three activities, which I will discuss individually.

Artistic Creativity in Christian Perspective

Human creativity is active in all human pursuits, but it has always, and rightly, been especially regarded as an attribute of the arts. For one thing, the arts are the province of the imagination, and the imagination is never limited solely to observable reality. Oscar Wilde once commented that art "has flowers that no forests know of, birds that no woodland possesses. . . . She can work miracles at her will, and when she calls monsters from the deep they come. She can bid the almond-tree blossom in winter, and send the snow upon the ripe cornfield."[8] Artists are the orators of the imagination. A work of art is a new creation that cannot be fully explained by any previously existing model.

In addition to the creative element of the arts, the related qualities of form, beauty, technique and craftsmanship are an essential ingredient of art. The elements of artistic form that all of the arts share are theme or centrality, pattern or design, organic unity (also called unity in variety or theme and variation), repetition or recurrence, rhythm, balance, contrast or tension, symmetry, harmony or "fittingness," unified progression and coherence. No single work of art needs to possess all of these, and some are more appropriately applied to one of the arts than the others. Nor should we limit these elements of artistic form to classical or Platonic aesthetic standards. Modern art also possesses its version of these formal qualities, even when artists claim that they are not using them.

The elements of artistic form are what the arts share. They differ in the medium by which they incarnate them. Music presents these elements of form through the medium of sound, literature through words, and painting through color, line and texture.

Artistic beauty or proficiency consists of the skillful composition and manipulation of the elements of aesthetic form. Such proficiency in the control of artistic technique is an important part of the value that we attach to the arts. Sometimes the creation of beauty is virtually the whole point of a work of art. This is especially true of much abstract or nonrepresentational art. Abstract art like the symmetrical designs of a Persian carpet or an ornamental wrought-iron railing or music without words have as their main purpose to present an artistic pattern for the pleasure of the beholder or listener.

And even in representational art, where part of the attention is focused on some aspect of human experience or external reality, the technical excellence remains an important part of the total effect. "Our primal aesthetical experience," writes one aesthetic theorist, is "a response of enchantment to 'beauty' (in a very wide sense of the term)."[9]

To gauge the importance of creativity and form in the artistic enterprise, we need only note the statements and practices of artists. They attribute creativity to a process of inspiration, however conceived. The revisions and refinements that they continue to lavish on their unfinished works are almost always directed toward a better crafted artistic form and rarely toward the ideational content of the work.

The poet Dylan Thomas wrote over 200 manuscript versions of his poem "Fern Hill." Beethoven sketched and resketched his compositions. Leonardo da Vinci drew a thousand hands. The Christian poet Gerard Manley Hopkins theorized that the purely artistic dimension of poetry exists "for its own sake and interest even over and above its interest of meaning."[10] And even when artistic excellence is not the main purpose of art, as when art is used in religious worship, for example, the formal beauty of a work enhances its effectiveness.

When we ask how the high value that the arts place on creativity and artistic form fits into a Christian world view, it is apparent at once that the two are in total accord. In contrast to much of the prevailing cultural climate of our time, biblical Christianity asserts that human creativity and artistry are not only desirable but indispensable.

The Doctrine of Creation. The starting point for thinking Christianly about creativity and beauty is the doctrine of creation, especially as described in the first chapter of the Bible. We learn in these verses that God himself is a creator who pronounced his handiwork "very good" (Gen 1:31). Equally important is the precise kind or nature of world that God created. It is a world that is beautiful as well as functional.

From a purely utilitarian point of view, God need not have created a world filled with symmetrical shapes and beautiful colors and pleasing sounds and varied textures. What we find in the visible creation is evidence not only of a functional mind but also an artistic imagination.

What kind of environment did God intend people to inhabit? Genesis 2:9 tells us: when God created Paradise, he "made to grow every tree that is pleasant to the sight and good for food." The conditions for human welfare are double—aesthetic and functional. Along with nature, the human arts have been the largest source of beauty in people's lives.

Not only did God create a universe filled with beautiful forms. He also created people in his own image (Gen 1:26-27). Exactly what does this mean? Theology has rightly stressed human rationality, morality and holiness as the things that people share with God. But in its narrative context in Genesis 1, where we first hear about God's image in people, something else is even more obvious, namely, the idea of creativity.

The classic study of what the image of God in people means to aesthetic theory is Dorothy L. Sayers' book *The Mind of the Maker*, where we read this regarding the Genesis statement about God's image in people:

Had the author of *Genesis* anything particular in his mind when he wrote? It is observable that in the passage leading up to the statement about man, he has given no detailed information about God. Looking at man, he sees in him something essentially divine, but when we turn back to see what he says about the original upon which the "image" of God was modeled, we find only the single assertion, "God created." The characteristic common to God and man is apparently that: the desire and the ability to make things.[11]

The image of the creative God in people is the theological reason why people create.

The doctrines of creation and the image of God in people affirm human creativity as something good in principle. Abraham Kuyper once wrote,

As image-bearer of God, man possesses the possibility both to create something beautiful, and to delight in it. . . . The world of sounds, the world of forms, the world of tints, and the world of poetic ideas, can have no source other than God; and it is our privilege as bearers of His image, to have a perception of this beautiful world, artistically to reproduce, and humanly to enjoy it.[12]

Can a Christian in good conscience do something as nonutilitarian as spending an afternoon at an art gallery or an evening at a concert? Can a student justify the time spent taking a course in fiction writing or painting or music composition? In a Christian scheme of things, the answer is clear: to be artistically creative, and to enter into the creativity of others, is to exercise the image of God within oneself.

The Doctrine of Stewardship. The Christian doctrine of stewardship leads to the same conclusion. A steward is a person put in charge of the resources of his or her master. Christian stewardship means serving God with the talents with which he has endowed us (see especially the parable of the talents in Mt 25:14-30). A duty of cultivation attaches to every ability and capacity that we possess.

What, then, are the talents with which God has endowed the creative artist? The classic answer is given in Exodus 31:3-5 in the description of the building of the tabernacle. We read that the Lord filled Bezalel "with the Spirit of God, with ability and intelligence, with knowledge and all craftsmanship, to devise artistic designs, to work in gold, silver, and bronze, in cutting stones for setting, and in carving wood, for work in every craft." These are the gifts of the artist. To cultivate them is to exercise stewardship. It is worthy of note, too, that "God called Bezalel" to exercise his creative ability (Ex 31:2). The creation and study and dissemination of art is a calling. The "creation mandate" that God gave to Adam and Eve when he told them to exercise dominion over the creation (Gen 1:26-30) is by extension also a cultural mandate to rule human culture in the name of God.

It is evident from what I have said that thinking Christianly about the arts involves rejection of the utilitarian mindset that scorns aesthetic form and beauty. The nonutilitarian aspect of the arts is not a mark against them. God did not create a purely utilitarian world. He filled his creation with much that is simply beautiful and delightful. When he created the perfect human environment, it included every tree that is pleasant to the sight (Gen 2:9). The garments of Aaron were embellished "for glory and for beauty" (Ex 28:2). We should note that well: beauty is worthy in itself, just as truth and goodness are.

The embellishments of the Temple served no architectural weightbearing function. They simply beautified the place. As H. R. Rookmaaker writes in his monograph *Art Needs No Justification*,

> God gave humanity the skill to make things beautiful, to make music, to write poems, to make sculpture, to decorate things. . . . Art has its own meaning. A work of art can stand in the art gallery and be cherished for its own sake. We listen to a piece of music simply to enjoy it.[13]

Art nearly always has a gratuitous, more-than-functional quality to it. By its very nature it involves a willingness to go beyond the purely utilitarian.

While it is an overstatement to attribute automatic moral effects to the arts, one of the virtues that the arts tend to foster is an inherent rejection of the materialism and acquisitiveness that are always threatening to overwhelm the human race. Because the enjoyment of artistic beauty is essentially nonutilitarian, it draws a boundary around human acquisitiveness and clears a ground in which people can recover and celebrate distinctively human values. Any world view that finds a place for artistic delight has a built-in curb against the purely acquisitive mindset that sees value only in practical activities that serve a utilitarian function.

Creativity and the Fall. We must, of course, not overstate the case for artistic creativity. Human creativity did not escape the effects of the Fall. Artistic creativity, too, is subject to moral and intellectual criticism. A painting or song or novel has no claim to our reverence or admiration simply because it is the product of human creativity. We must differentiate between noble and ignoble manifestations of the creative impulse.

One criterion is the purpose or *telos* that governs an artist's effort. Art composed to feed an artist's greed for fame or wealth has a less noble purpose than art designed to serve one's fellow humans or to glorify God. Art that caters to the coarse taste for pornography is less worthy than creativity that aims to dignify and refine human taste.

Another criterion for judging the worthiness of human creativity is the effect of art on its audience. We rightly admire art, music and literature whose effect is to make people more sensitive, moral or humanly refined. And we should judge negatively art whose effect is to encourage people to behave selfishly, immorally or coarsely.

Yet another standard by which we can judge artistic creativity is aesthetic excellence. Poorly executed paintings or musical compositions or stories might be the products of someone's creativity, but they do not for that reason merit our admiration. Technical excellence, on the other hand, is one of the very aims of artistic creativity. We might note, therefore, that the Christian content of a work of art that is technically mediocre does not redeem the work as a piece of creativity. In fact, the lack of artistic excellence detracts from the impact of the Christian content.

Artistic creativity is a great gift, but it is not inherently sacred or good. For at least a century now, non-Christian enthusiasts for the arts have tended to find in art a substitute for the Christian religion. Nietzsche virtually deified free creativity. The romantic poets regarded the imagination as the religious faculty by which we have contact with the supernatural. Such people elevate the imagination to a religious role that the Bible reserves for a person's "heart" or "soul."

Artistic creativity can never hold such an esteemed place in a Christian world view. There is wisdom and beauty but not salvation in a sonnet. Art can satisfy some of the same longings that religion does. It speaks to the human capacity for illumination, mystery, order and beauty. But a Christian finds the ultimate satisfaction of these longings in God, not in art. It is this conviction that lies behind the statement of C. S. Lewis that

> the Christian will take literature a little less seriously than the cultured Pagan. . . . The unbeliever is always apt to make a kind of religion of his aesthetic experiences. . . . But the Christian knows from the outset that the salvation of a single soul is more important than the production and preservation of all the epics and tragedies in the world.[14]

The Christian religion encourages a balanced view toward artistic creativity. To a technological world that values only what is utilitarian, Christianity declares that whatever is beautiful, whether it is a tree or a sonata, has worth in itself because a creative God has conferred the capacity for artistry on his human creatures. To enthusiasts for the arts who make an idol of the imagination and its products, Christianity asserts that God the Creator is always separate from his creation, whether nature or culture.

The Portrayal of Human Experience in the Arts

The arts take human experience as their subject. They are above all the expression of human *response* to reality. When a painter paints a landscape, he or she is suggesting something of the human response to nature. Music is particularly adept at expressing the inner weather of the human emotions or condition.

Literature is even more comprehensive in its ability to present the contours of human experience in the world. The novelist Joseph Conrad wrote, "My task . . . is, by the power of the written word to make you hear, to make you feel—it is, before all, to make you *see*."[15] So rooted are the arts in reality that the oldest and most influential of all aesthetic theories has regarded the arts as an imitation of reality.

Creative artists are sensitive observers of reality. "The writer should never be ashamed of staring," writes novelist Flannery O'Connor.[16] The American painter Andrew Wyeth once told an interviewer, "I love to study the many things that grow below the corn stalks and bring them back into the studio to study the color. If one could only catch that true color of nature—the very thought of it drives me mad."[17] The creative artist's vocation is to stare at the created and human worlds and to lure the rest of us into a similar act of contemplation.

The arts stay close to the way things are in the world. The knowledge that they convey is an experiential knowledge of the physical and human worlds. Whether or not this is a knowledge worth having depends on one's values and world view. Plato viewed such knowledge as rather frivolous, a knowledge hardly worth having.

A Christian viewpoint disagrees with this denigration of physical and human reality. It does so partly on the basis of the doctrine of creation. Things are real because God made them. And because he made them, they are worthy of study and celebration and love. Not only did God make things. He created people in such a way that they perceive them as much through their physical senses as their minds. The color and smell of a rose are not irrelevant or illusory.

The Christian doctrine of Incarnation points in the same direction. When Jesus took on human form in order to redeem people, he demonstrated that earthly, human experience is of immense worth. Christianity is not escapist. It does not substitute a heavenly world for the earthly one. It brings a spiritual reality *into* the earthly order.

Simply at the level of subject matter, then, the Christian doctrines of creation and Incarnation have far-reaching implications for the arts. Visual artists are assured that their preoccupation with the scenes and people and colors that they paint or mold are worthy of such attention. Musicians need not doubt the significance of the human feelings and attitudes embodied in their sounds. Poets and storytellers and dramatists can be convinced that their portrayal of the whole range of human experience in the natural and social worlds is a worthwhile endeavor. Christian artists can take all of life as their subject, just as the writers of the Bible did.

Values and Reality: The Artist's Perspective. We might think that the mere subject matter of an artistic work is philosophically neutral and that perspective enters only when artists add their interpretive slant to the subject of portrayal. But the world view of creative artists emerges even from the subjects they select for portrayal. The details that an artist includes in the limited confines of a single work carry a burden of meaning larger than themselves and are understood to be representative of a bigger sense of life. Artistic subject matter implies a statement about both values and reality.

In the realm of *values,* artists imply what they regard as worthy of human attention whenever they put brush to canvas or pen to paper. Why did the French painter Courbet shock the artistic norms of his day by painting common stonebreakers and a peasant burial? Because his very choice of such subject matter implied that true worth resides in people of humble social standing instead of people with aristocratic status. Bach wrote church music on sacred themes because he valued supremely the worship of God. Wordsworth's nature poems, simply at the level of subject matter, express his attitude toward what is important in human experience.

What an artist chooses to portray is a comment about *reality* as well as values. Artists create out of the habitual furniture of their minds. What they exclude is as important as what they include. Writers whose poems or stories never portray God, spiritual reality or Christian values exhibit, simply at the level of subject matter, a secular world view. We can tell by looking at the table of contents of the works of Mendelssohn and Handel that their view of reality was Christian. Flannery O'Connor theorized that "it is from the kind of world the writer creates, from the kind of character and detail he invests it with, that a reader can find the intellectual meaning of a book."[18]

We might think that abstract or nonrepresentational art and music are free from perspective, but they, too, are an implied comment about reality. A symphony in which organization dominates the composition conveys a different sense of life from a symphony in which disorganization dominates. A vastly different world view emerges from the intricate harmony of a Persian tapestry and most modern abstract art. When a graduate student who works in abstract sculpture recently had his work critiqued by his department, he was asked why his nonrepresentational sculptures possessed an order and gracefulness and clean lines so atypical ot prevailing contemporary trends. His answer was that his sculpture expressed his Christian view of the world as ultimately orderly.

Artistic content is inherently laden with perspective. Christians have a picture of reality and a value system stemming from their Christian world view. As they assimilate works of art, therefore, they should self-consciously assess the adequacy of artistic pictures of the world in terms of a Christian framework. The central tenets in that world view are the existence of God and an unseen spiritual world, the worth of physical reality, the value of the individual person and social institutions, the fact of human evil and fallenness, the availability of God's redemptive grace, and a view of human history as being under God's purposeful providence and headed toward a goal.

As Christians look at the subject matter of artistic works through the lens of their convictions, some of what they see comes into focus. Other objects remain out of focus. In either case, art has served its useful purpose: it has furnished the recipient with an occasion to exercise intellectual discrimination on questions of values and reality. Some value systems and views of reality are wrong, but Christians have an obligation to understand the world in which they live and to which they minister.

The Interpretation of Reality in Works of Art

Artists do more than present human experience; they also *interpret* it from a specific perspective. Works of art make implied assertions about reality. This is simply one of the conventions with which people approach the artistic enterprise, whether as creators or recipients. The primary convention of the arts is what aesthetic theorist Jonathan Culler calls "the rule of significance," meaning that we should look on works of art "as expressing a significant attitude to some problem concerning man and/or his relation to the universe."[19] Artists intend meanings, and audiences can scarcely avoid looking for them.

Art's Implied Assertions. Works of art make implied assertions, just as history and science and philosophy do. For convenience, we can say that the arts make implied claims about the three great issues of life:

1. Reality: what really exists, and what is its nature?
2. Morality: what constitutes right and wrong behavior?
3. Values: what really matters, and what matters most and least?

For purposes of illustration, I turn first to a pair of nineteenth-century English painters, Constable and Turner. They both chose nature as their major subject. Looking at a selection of their paintings convinces us not simply that physical nature is an important part of reality but also that it is something of great worth in human experience.

But along with these similarities we notice obvious differences in how Constable and Turner interpreted nature. What do we see as we look at Constable's famous paintings of Salisbury Cathedral? We see the beauty and harmony of nature. We see nature in a religious light and as the friend of people. The human and natural worlds are unified. Constable himself said that he painted nature as benevolent because he sensed God's presence in nature.

Turner offers quite a different interpretation of nature. His colors are more intense, his brush strokes much broader and more passionate. There is an element of terror in many of his nature scenes. One of his paintings shows a gigantic avalanche ready to overwhelm a matchbox cabin under its furious weight. In such a painting nature is not nurturing, as in Constable and the Dutch realists, but hostile. The one is not necessarily more Christian than the other, though we should not minimize how artists select details that suggest their overall view of human possibilities in the universe.

For a literary illustration, consider the following sonnet, entitled "God's Grandeur," by Gerard Manley Hopkins:

The world is charged with the grandeur of God.
  It will flame out, like shining from shook foil.
  It gathers to a greatness, like the ooze of oil
Crushed. Why do men then now not reck his rod?
Generations have trod, have trod, have trod;
  And all is seared with trade; bleared, smeared with toil;
  And wears man's smudge and shares man's smell: the soil
Is bare now, nor can foot feel, being shod.

And for all this, nature is never spent;
  There lives the dearest freshness deep down things;
And though the last lights off the black West went
  Oh, morning, at the brown brink eastward, springs—
Because the Holy Ghost over the bent
  World broods with warm breast and with ah! bright wings.

The subject of the poem is the permanent freshness of nature. The perspective from which we view that reality is the grandeur of God. What really exists? According to this poem, the physical world of sun and trees and the spiritual world that includes the triune God are equally real. What constitutes moral and immoral behavior? To live morally is to live in reverence before God's creation. To desecrate nature in pursuit of selfish acquisitiveness is immoral. What values are most worthy of human pursuit? God and nature.

The Audience's Responsibility. If works of art are this laden with meaning, what are the implications for those who constitute the audience of the arts? It is today a commonplace that we appropriate works of art in terms of our own values, morality and view of reality. A Christian world view asserts specific ideas in all three areas. To assimilate the arts in a Christian way means to interact with their implied assertions within a framework of Christian doctrine, as derived from the Bible.

Because the three big subject areas of the arts are God, people and nature, it is especially crucial for Christians to have a grasp of Christian truth about these topics whenever they encounter works of art. In a Christian view, God is the ultimate reality and object of devotion. God is the one who has created everything that exists in the universe. Several important corollaries follow. One is that God is transcendent over reality and never to be equated with the creation. Another is that since God is the ultimate source and end of reality, everything else derives its identity from God. Thus people are the creatures of God, moral goodness consists of doing God's will, history is the outworking of God's purposes, human institutions such as state and family are ordained by God, and so forth.

Christianity postulates a threefold view of people: good and worthy in principle because God made them in his image, evil or fallen by virtue of their sinful actions, and capable of restoration by God's grace. Judged by such a standard, any view of people is inadequate if it sees them as *only* evil or *only* good. In a Christian scheme, people are evil by their inclinations but good as they participate in God's grace. In either case, human choice is both possible and necessary. A lot of art is *truthful* without telling the whole *truth*. It accurately portrays part of the truth about human nature, but still falls short of a Christian perspective because it fails to do justice to the comprehensive balance in a Christian view of people.

The Christian view of nature runs parallel to the view of people. Nature was created by God and is under his providential control. This means on the one hand that nature itself is not divine and on the other that it is worthy of love and reverence. A lot of artistic portrayal of nature errs in either overvaluing or undervaluing it. Medieval painting and music were so preoccupied with heaven and angels and Madonnas and grace that they suffer from an unbiblical denigration of nature. The reverse has been true of the arts during the last two centuries.

At the heart of the Christian world view is a balance or tension between good and evil, hope and despair, optimism and pessimism. Is a work of art unchristian in its viewpoint if it portrays only a sense of despair or discord? Isn't the Fall a keystone of Christian doctrine? If so, why should Christians not endorse the protest music and literature and painting that are so dominant in the twentieth century?

The best framework that I have seen for grappling with this issue is Francis Schaeffer's commonsensical suggestion that Christianity consists of two themes.[20] One is the pessimistic fact of sin, despair and lostness in human experience. The other theme is the hope, meaningfulness and redemptive potential in life. A Christian world view embraces both halves of this tension. The sense of life that emerges from artistic works is less than Christian if it omits either side of the tension. The garbage can behind the house and the rose bush in front of the house are equally real.

To summarize, artists inevitably offer a perspective on such basic human issues as what really exists, how people should act and what values are worthy of human devotion. The obligation of Christian artists is to convey a Christian viewpoint in their stories and paintings and musical compositions. The task of all Christians is to discern and evaluate the perspectives that artists offer for their approval whenever they read or look or listen.

Truth in Art

We are now in a position to consider the question that inevitably arises when art is considered in terms of world view. Do the arts tell the truth? There is no single answer to the question because there are various types or levels of truth in art. There is a range of ways in which a work of art can be true or false. I will discuss them under the headings of human values, representational truth and ideational or perspectival truth.

Human Values. To begin, the arts as a whole tell us the truth about what is foundational in human experience. Simply at the level of content, the arts keep calling us back to bedrock humanity. The arts are probably the most accurate index to human preoccupations, values, fears and longings that we possess. If we wish to know what people want and do not want, we can go to their stories and poems and songs ana paintings.

This is why we often feel that we have learned more from art than from life. In real life the essential patterns and values are usually obscured by the sheer complexity and pressures of living. The arts, however, awaken our awareness of the central realities of human experience—realities such as nature and God and family and love and pain. A work of art is a distillation of experience in which the irrelevancies are stripped away. The knowledge that the arts give us is rarely new information but rather a bringing to consciousness of what we already know but to which we become oblivious in daily living.

The arts are therefore a great organizing force in human life. When people say that the arts help them to understand or make sense of life, they usually mean the ability of the arts to cut through the clutter and put them in touch with what is enduring in human experience. This, then, is one level of truth in the arts: truthfulness to the fears, longings and values of the human race. The arts possess such truth regardless of the philosophical perspective of an artist. Such knowledge about human experience is a type of truth that Christians need; it is one of their bonds with the human race.

Representational Truth. A second level of truth in the arts is representational truth, by which I mean truthfulness to the way things are in the world. Artists are sensitive observers of reality. They present human experience in their chosen artistic medium. Whenever a writer or composer or visual artist accurately captures the contours of human experience or external reality, we can say that the resulting work of art is true to reality.

A work of art can be true at this level even though the perspective from which the subject is viewed might be wrong. As with the previous level of truth (art as a truthful repository of what is most essential in human experience), we can make very large claims for the truth of art in its faithfulness to reality. We have all looked at paintings or read stories and poems that struck us as false to reality, to the way things are, but the overwhelming majority of art is true to reality.

Of course the arts are not "photographically" real. They use artistic techniques of highlighting, selectivity, omission, juxtaposition and distortion in their portrayal of reality. There is a certain indirection to art. Thus the "truthfulness" of a painted portrait of a person is not measured in terms of photographic realism but in terms of whether it captures the reality of grief or serenity or the beauty of the human face. Coleridge's *Rime of the Ancient Mariner* contains such fantastic elements as ghosts and surrealistic landscapes and an albatross with supernatural powers. But these elements of fantasy accurately suggest such realities as sin, guilt, alienation and renewal. The imaginative details in a work of art are a lens or window through which we look at life.

Perspectival Truth. The third level at which the truthfulness of a work of art needs to be tested is the level of perspective or implied assertion. I noted earlier that artists inevitably offer an interpretation of the human experiences that they portray. Not all art forms are equally laden with perspective. Literature, because it consists of words, is the most consistently perspectival. Music, being the most nonrepresentational, is least likely to bear ideational perspective. The visual arts fall somewhere between the two.

The perspectives or themes embodied in artistic works range from a general sense of life at one end of the spectrum to very specific assertions at the other. At the general end, artistic perspective consists of such attitudes as order or lack of it, hope or despair, the presence or absence of a supernatural reality, meaning or futility. As works of art become more explicitly laden with perspective, they embody specific ideas about God, people, society and nature, or about what constitutes good and bad behavior, or about what values are worthy and unworthy of human devotion.

As people assimilate a work of art, they do so in terms of their own world view. They measure the perspective in works of art by their own convictions. The more committed they are to a standard of truth that they regard as authoritative, the more consciously they are likely to assess what they encounter in art in terms of their own world view.

Two-Stage Criticism. Christians surely fall into the category of people committed to a standard of truth. The methodology for integrating one's encounter with works of art and one's Christian faith has been succinctly summarized in T. S. Eliot's theory that the criticism of artistic works

> should be completed by criticism from a definite ethical and theological standpoint. . . . It is . . . necessary for [Christians] to scrutinize . . . works of imagination with explicit ethical and theological standards. . . . What I believe to be incumbent upon all Christians is the duty of maintaining consciously certain standards and criteria of criticism over and above those applied by the rest of the world; and that by these criteria and standards everything . . . must be tested.[21]

Notice that Eliot envisions a two-stage process of criticism. *First* we must receive the work on its own terms and allow it to say what it really says. *Then* we must exercise our prerogative of agreeing or disagreeing with the artist's interpretation of reality and experience.

What are the "explicit ethical and theological standards" by which Eliot thinks Christians should assess the truth content of art? They are based ultimately on the Bible, the only final authority for belief in what is, after all, a *revealed* religion. The insights of Christian creeds based on the Bible and Christian thinkers who are gifted to codify and state the implications of biblical doctrine become important elements in a person's understanding of a Christian world view. In the application of Christian doctrine to specific artistic assertions about life, biblical revelation obviously needs to be supplemented by human reason in any Christian critique of art.

Judging the truthfulness of the implied assertions of art is a form of intellectually testing the spirits to see if they are from God. The criteria by which the ideational or perspectival truth of art is judged are the same intellectual standards as apply to the other disciplines. The arts, for all their beauty and delightfulness and imaginative power, do not allow us to take a holiday from the mind. The task of completing artistic criticism with a Christian assessment of an artist's perspective or world view needs to be informed by insights from philosophy, theology, ethics and psychology. It can never rest solely on aesthetic considerations.

Common Grace. The truthfulness of a work of art does not depend on an artist's Christian orthodoxy. The doctrine of common grace is one of the most important ingredients in a Christian approach to the study and appreciation of the arts. The doctrine of common grace asserts that God endows all people, believers and unbelievers alike, with a capacity for goodness, truth, creativity and so forth. All truth is God's truth. It is not suspect if it happens to be expressed by non-Christian artists.

The Bible itself affirms that unbelieving artists can express truth. In the New Testament, Paul several times quotes with approval from pagan Greek poets.[22] When Solomon needed visual artists who could express the beauty of holiness, he hired the best available artists, who happened to be pagans.[23] As John Calvin wrote regarding the application of the doctrine of common grace to the arts, "All truth is from God; and consequently, if wicked men have said anything that is true and just, we ought not to reject it; for it has come from God."[24]

Does art tell the truth? There is no single answer to the perennial question. A lot of misleading eulogistic overstatements and denigrating understatements have been made about the truthfulness of art by people who ignore the range of ways in which art can be true and false.

Virtually all art tells us the truth about the foundational preoccupations, values, fears and longings of the human race. Most art is true as a representation of some aspect of human experience or external reality. At the level of intellectual perspective or interpretation of reality, most of the world's art, music and literature has not measured up to a Christian standard of truth.

Of course it is possible to state the theme of a work of art so broadly that virtually no one, including Christians, would disagree with the statement. But when pressed more specifically at the level of implied philosophical assertion, most art through the centuries has deviated from Christian doctrine, despite the predominantly Christian tenor of European culture during the Middle Ages and Renaissance.

Not all art is Christian in viewpoint, but it is always of interest to Christians because it clarifies the human situation to which the Christian faith speaks. Encountering the moral and philosophic viewpoints of artistic works is an avenue to understanding the people with whom we live and the culture that is our daily environment. Measuring those viewpoints by a Christian norm serves as an invaluable catalyst to a Christian's thinking about human issues.

Why Christians Need the Arts

The arts serve many functions in human culture. They are functions that Christians should welcome and that they avoid to their own harm.

One of the functions of art can be summed up under such related words as refreshment, recreation, entertainment and the enjoyment of artistic form or beauty. The arts are a celebration of life. The goal of our excursions into the realm of imaginative art is to send us back to real life with a renewed zest for it. The arts awaken us to the hidden beauty of the world and are themselves an extension of that beauty. The arts affirm the humanness of humans. Even when the subject of art is human evil and suffering and ugliness, the artistic skill with which the subject is rendered is a tribute to human achievement.

The arts are useful as well as delightful. They are a great ordering force in human culture. As the arts present human experience for our contemplation, they intensify our involvement with life, heighten our awareness, expand our range of experiences, and enlarge our human sympathies and compassion. The arts sharpen and reward the senses and do justice to the emotional and imagining side of human nature. They give shape to our own experiences, thereby satisfying the human urge for adequate expression of insights and feelings.

Because the arts are interpretive in nature, they speak to our intellect. They offer a diagnosis, definition and explanation for the human condition. With their implied assertions about life, the arts force us to think, to ponder alternative views of life, to commit ourselves to our own convictions of truth. They provide the materials for us to exercise and expand our own angle of vision.

These are the gifts of art. They are even more important to Christians than to non-Christians because to the human reasons for art a Christian can add an even more ultimate rationale—the glory of God. This, indeed, is the appointed consummation of the arts. The person who can revere the ultimate source and end of human creativity has an added reason to cherish the ability of the arts to intensify human awareness and compassion, to enhance human enjoyment and understanding.

Afterword

A world view, with its beliefs and attitudes and values, affords an integrating framework for all we do. A Christian world view, then, affects theoretical thinking, professional and business practices, aesthetic activity and public policy, as well as the more mundane features of everyday life. To change the metaphor, it provides perspective, an all-embracing point of view with which to come at whatever the task may be.

The preceding chapters are merely samples, drawn from the humanities and from the natural and behavioral sciences. Volumes have been written in each of the areas we have addressed, and further volumes in areas we have omitted; the life sciences and social sciences, philosophy and education are every bit as important to the Christian mind as psychology, physics, art and history. In every area of learning, a Christian world view speaks.

In the marketplace of ideas, not only in academia but also in the public arena and the business and professional worlds, a Christian view of things must find clear, cogent and captivating expression. All of us bear this responsibility. In a real sense the marketplace of ideas operates within each of our minds, and there too Christian thinking must find clear, captivating expression, cogent too if we are to communicate effectively to others.

To get started into this territory we need to identify some "ports of entry" that are readily accessible. In what follows I suggest four such starting points as an agenda for the Christian mind.

Historical Precedents. Christianity has for nearly two thousand years been addressing the varied scope of human life and learning. It would therefore be the height of presumption to suppose we either could or should start afresh in our generation. Three of the preceding essays drew extensively on historical precedents, not to photocopy for our day what others did for theirs, but rather to see how they addressed situations analagous to our own and to build on their contributions. A history of Christian involvement exists in all of the arts and sciences, as well as politics and commerce. One can do little better for a start than to read Christian thinkers and artists and scientists and statesmen from the past, and to ask how their kind of creative work might be attempted in our day.

Theoretical Foundations. Any systematic development of the Christian mind will require identifying beliefs and values that have a formative role in the overall framework of a world view. Theological concepts, like the sort which the opening essay develops and which the others draw on too, are therefore crucial. We need a biblical understanding of God as Creator and Lord of all, and of our place as persons bearing God's image, in creation, sin and redemption. These will undergird, indeed they give rise to, a Christian view of art or science, work or play, or anything.

Theological foundations function formatively, but philosophical foundations too are involved. A Christian philosophy of art is needed to take stock of aesthetic theories and to work out the implications of Christian belief in this area. The same is true of the philosophy of science, as Joseph Spradley's essay makes plain, and of history, politics and so forth. Philosophy is foundational to any world view in that it focuses on the nature of knowledge and belief, on the kinds of reality with which we are involved, on the value judgments we make in any area of thought. The unexamined life, said Socrates, is not worth living; certainly in the marketplace of ideas, unexamined beliefs and values are not worth marketing. Theoretical foundations, properly conceived and carefully scrutinized, are crucial. Hence the importance of good theology and careful philosophical work.

Ethical Issues. In his essay on psychology, Kirk Farnsworth points to moral problems in scientific research and professional practice. In the last decades, business, politics, medicine and environmental studies have also been the subject of moral concern. This should not surprise us, if we take the Christian doctrine of sin seriously. Nor on the other hand should we be surprised at the widespread criticism that unethical practices receive, if we keep in mind that the common grace of God preserves us from doing the worst of which we are capable. Yet the Christian of all people, touched by God's saving grace as well, should be doubly concerned about ethical issues wherever they arise. A Christian world view provides a framework for both ethical thinking and social action.

The God of justice and love calls us to do justice, to love kindness and to walk humbly before God (Mic 6:8). This is the stuff of which social reform is made, reform that furthers economic justice, that cares for the poor and the oppressed. It is also the stuff of moral integrity and right attitudes in any walk of life. It mandates our attention to ethical issues: business and bioethics, environmental and research ethics, professional ethics in any field.

Mandates and Priorities. Within the framework of a Christian world view, we have seen a mandate for the Christian to work in art and science and psychology, and any morally legitimate human endeavor. This mandate sets priorities that may run counter to those prevailing in the academic world or in society at large today. The overall mandate is in relation to God, to see life as a glad and worshipful response to its Maker, and to do this by serving others with the varied resources God provides. What Jesus called the first and great commandment, and the second that is like unto it (Mt 22:34-40), speaks articulately to that. Particular priorities must be adjusted accordingly. For the scholar, this may mean choosing a research topic for its potentially strategic contribution, in preference to one that ensures professional advancement. For the businessperson it may mean identifying real needs to be met, rather than catering to needs artificially created by manipulative advertising. It will mean ensuring that one's family is not neglected through professional involvement. Priorities for both thought and action must be assessed within the overall life mandate implicit in a Christian world view.

This shaping of a Christian mind is not an isolated goal, important as it may be in God's redemption of the whole person. To shape a Christian mind is to shape the history of the church in today's and tomorrow's world. To shape the church's influence is to shape history itself. If there is anything at all to the adage that ideas shape history, it is also true that God shapes history through capturing the mind for Christ.

Arthur F. Holmes

Notes

Chapter One: Toward a Christian View of Things

[1]Charles Malik, *The Two Tasks* (Westchester, Ill.: Cornerstone Books, 1980). See also Arnold Nash, *The University and the Modern World* (London: Macmillan, 1944).

[2]This theme is developed in A. F. Holmes, *All Truth Is God's Truth* (1977; reprint ed., Downers Grove, Ill.: InterVarsity Press, 1983).

[3]See the "Christian Philosophy" article in *Encyclopaedia Britannica,* 15th ed., 1974.

[4]Nicholas Wolterstorff, *Reason Within the Bounds of Religion* (Grand Rapids: Eerdmans, 1976).

[5]This realization poses questions about the justification of belief and the adoption of one world view over against others. On this epistemological issue, see David L. Wolfe, *Epistemology* (Downers Grove, Ill.: InterVarsity Press, 1982).

[6]For more on this topic, see A. F. Holmes, *Ethics: Approaching Moral Decisions* (Downers Grove, Ill.: InterVarsity Press, 1984), chap. 7.

[7]The topics covered in this essay are explored more fully in A. F. Holmes, *Contours of a World View* (Grand Rapids: Eerdmans, 1983); Harry Blamires, *The Christian Mind* (1963; reprint ed., Ann Arbor: Servant Books, 1978); J. Langdon Gilkey, *Maker of Heaven and Earth* (New York: Doubleday, 1959); and an 1898 classic by Abraham Kuyper, *Lectures on Calvinism* (Grand Rapids: Eerdmans, 1931).

Chapter Two: Christian World Views and Some Lessons of History

[1]For a general picture of the American situation, see *Eerdmans' Handbook to Christianity in America* (Grand Rapids: Eerdmans, 1983); and for more particular consideration of how the American setting has affected Christian thinking, see Nathan O. Hatch, "Evangelicalism as a Democratic Movement," in *Evangelicals and Modern America,* ed. George M. Marsden (Grand Rapids: Eerdmans, 1984).

[2]On meanings associated with biblical language and concepts, see William Barclay, *New Testament Words* (Philadelphia: Westminster, 1964); and Colin Brown, ed., *The*

New International Dictionary of New Testament Theology (Grand Rapids: Zondervan, 1975-78), both of which also consider the conceptual legacy of the Old Testament.

[3]See J. N. D. Kelly, *Early Christian Doctrines*, 2nd ed. (New York: Harper & Row, 1960); and Jaroslav Pelikan, *The Emergence of the Catholic Tradition (100-600)* (Chicago: University of Chicago Press, 1971).

[4]Brian Tierney, ed., *The Middle Ages*, vol. 1., *Sources of Medieval History* (New York: Knopf, 1970), p. 76; and more generally on monasticism, David Knowles, *The Middle Ages* (New York: Paulist, 1969).

[5]G. K. Chesterton, *Saint Thomas Aquinas* (Garden City, N.Y.: Doubleday, 1956), p. 105; and more generally, Ralph McInerny, *Saint Thomas Aquinas* (Boston: G. K. Hall, 1977).

[6]An excellent description of how scholarship flourished in the Reformation age among both Catholics and Protestants is E. Harris Harbison, *The Christian Scholar in the Age of the Reformation* (reprinted; Grand Rapids: Eerdmans, 1983); and more particularly for the challenge to education, Mark A. Noll, "The Earliest Protestants and the Reformation of Education," *Westminster Theological Journal* 43 (1980):97-131.

[7]See T. H. L. Parker, *John Calvin: A Biography* (Philadelphia: Westminster, 1975); John T. McNeill, *The History and Character of Calvinism* (New York: Oxford University Press, 1954); and W. Stanford Reid, ed., *John Calvin: His Influence in the Western World* (Grand Rapids: Zondervan, 1982).

[8]See Steven Runciman, *The Medieval Manichee* (Cambridge, Eng.: Cambridge University Press, 1947).

[9]The best studies in English are by F. Ernest Stoeffler, *The Rise of Evangelical Pietism* (Leiden: E. J. Brill, 1965); and *German Pietism during the Eighteenth Century* (Leiden: E. J. Brill, 1973).

[10]See Franklin L. Baumer, *Modern European Thought: Continuity and Change in Ideas, 1600-1950* (New York: Macmillan, 1977), with special attention to sections on romanticism and the discussion of Immanuel Kant and F. D. E. Schleiermacher.

[11]For a general picture, see Henry F. May, *The Enlightenment in America* (New York: Oxford University Press, 1976).

[12]See Wallace Anderson, ed., *Scientific and Philosophical Writings: The Works of Jonathan Edwards*, vol. 6 (New Haven: Yale University Press, 1980); and Norman Fiering, *Jonathan Edwards's Moral Thought and Its British Context* (Chapel Hill: University of North Carolina Press, 1981).

[13]A fuller discussion of this development is found in Mark A. Noll, George M. Marsden and Nathan O. Hatch, *The Search for Christian America* (Westchester, Ill.: Crossway, 1983).

[14]See Sydney E. Ahlstrom, *A Religious History of the American People* (New Haven: Yale University Press, 1972), pp. 403-90.

[15]See especially George M. Marsden, "The Collapse of American Evangelical Academia," in *Faith and Rationality*, eds. Alvin Plantinga and Nicholas Wolterstorff (Notre Dame, Ind.: University of Notre Dame Press, 1983); and for additional

details, Mark A. Noll, "Christian Thinking and the Rise of the American University," *Christian Scholar's Review* 9 (1979):3-16.

16The contrasting patterns are well described in William R. Hutchison, *The Modernist Impulse in American Protestantism* (Cambridge, Mass.: Harvard University Press, 1976); and George M. Marsden, *Fundamentalism and American Culture: The Shaping of Twentieth-Century Evangelicalism 1870-1925* (New York: Oxford University Press, 1980).

17See George H. Williams, *The Mind of John Paul II* (New York: Seabury, 1981).

18As examples of this work, see G. K. Chesterton, *Orthodoxy* (Garden City, N.Y.: Doubleday, 1973), and *The Everlasting Man* (Garden City, N.Y.: Doubleday, 1974); and Malcolm Muggeridge, *Jesus Rediscovered* (Garden City, N.Y.: Doubleday, 1979), and *Chronicles of Wasted Time* (New York: Morrow, 1973-).

19See as examples, C. S. Lewis, *Mere Christianity* (New York: Macmillan, 1964), and *God in the Dock: Essays on Theology and Ethics* (Grand Rapids: Eerdmans, 1970). Others from Britain who call for similar commitments are Os Guinness, *The Dust of Death* (Downers Grove, Ill.: InterVarsity Press, 1972); and Harry Blamires, *The Christian Mind* (New York: Seabury, 1963).

20As examples, see Carl F. H. Henry, *Christian Personal Ethics* (Grand Rapids: Eerdmans, 1957); as ed., *Horizons of Science* (San Francisco: Harper and Row, 1978); C. Stephen Evans, *Preserving the Person: A Look at the Human Sciences* (Downers Grove, Ill.: InterVarsity Press, 1977); Plantinga and Wolterstorff, *Faith and Rationality*, 1983; Robert D. Linder and Richard V. Pierard, *Politics: A Case for Christian Action* (Downers Grove, Ill.: InterVarsity Press, 1973); and Francis Schaeffer, *Escape from Reason* (Downers Grove, Ill.: InterVarsity Press, 1968).

Chapter Three: A Christian View of the Physical World

1John William Draper, *The Conflict between Religion and Science*, 7th ed. (London: Henry S. King, 1876); Andrew Dickson White, *A History of the Warfare of Science and Theology in Christendom*, 2 vols. (New York: Appleton, 1896).

2See David C. Lindberg, "Science and the Early Christian Church," *Isis* 74 (1983):509-30, for a discussion of this claim.

3James R. Moore, *The Post-Darwinian Controversies* (Cambridge, Eng.: Cambridge University Press, 1979).

4Arthur Holmes, *Contours of a World View* (Grand Rapids: Eerdmans, 1983), chap. 3.

5C. S. Lewis, *The Abolition of Man* (New York: Macmillan, 1947).

6Barry Commoner, *The Closing Circle* (New York: Knopf, 1971); Theodore Roszak, *Where the Wasteland Ends* (Garden City, N.Y.: Doubleday, 1971).

7Norwood Russell Hanson, *Patterns of Discovery* (Cambridge, Eng.: Cambridge University Press, 1958).

8Thomas Kuhn, *The Structure of Scientific Revolutions* (Chicago: University of Chicago Press, 1962).

9Herbert Butterfield, *The Origins of Modern Science* (New York: Free Press, 1965), chap. 4.

10Claus Westermann, *The Genesis Account of Creation* (Philadelphia: Fortress, 1964).

11Harvey Cox, *The Secular City* (New York: Macmillan, 1965), chap. 1.

12Gilkey, *Maker of Heaven and Earth*; Daniel O'Connor and Francis Oakley, eds., *Creation: The Impact of an Idea* (New York: Scribners, 1969), see especially articles by M. Foster.

13Ronald Youngblood, *How It All Began* (Ventura, Calif.: Regal, 1980).

14Augustine *City of God* 12. 4.

15Oscar Cullmann, *Immortality of the Soul or Resurrection of the Dead?* (London: Epworth, 1958).

16R. Hooykaas, *Religion and the Rise of Modern Science* (Grand Rapids, Mich.: Eerdmans, 1972).

17Alfred North Whitehead, *Science and the Modern World* (New York: Macmillan, 1925), p. 12.

18Eugene M. Klaaren, *Religious Origins of Modern Science* (Grand Rapids: Eerdmans, 1977).

19Isaac Newton, *Mathematical Principles of Natural Philosophy*, translated by Andrew Motte (1729), revised by Cajori (Berkeley: University of California Press, 1934), concluding General Scholium.

20Thomas Derr, *Ecology and Human Need* (Philadelphia: Westminster Press, 1973); Lauren Wilkinson, ed., *Earthkeeping* (Grand Rapids: Eerdmans, 1980).

21Oscar Cullmann, *Christ and Time* (Philadelphia: Westminster Press, 1952).

22Gilkey, *Maker of Heaven and Earth*, chap. 9.

23Max Weber, *The Protestant Ethic and the Spirit of Capitalism* (New York: Scribners, 1958).

24John Dillenberger, *Protestant Thought and Natural Science* (New York: Doubleday, 1960); Robert K. Merton, *Science, Technology, and Society in Seventeenth Century England* (New York: Harper Torchbooks, 1970).

25Robert Jastrow, *God and the Astronomers* (New York: W. W. Norton, 1978), pp. 105-6.

26E. L. Mascall, *Christian Theology and Natural Science* (New York: Ronald, 1956).

27Bernard Ramm, *The Christian View of Science and Scripture* (Grand Rapids: Eerdmans, 1955).

28Ian Barbour, *Issues in Science and Religion* (New York: Prentice-Hall, 1966), p. 132.

29Ibid., p. 163.

30Michael Polanyi, *Personal Knowledge* (Chicago: University of Chicago Press, 1958).

31William G. Pollard, *Chance and Providence* (New York: Scribners, 1958).

32Richard Bube, *The Human Quest* (Waco, Tex: Word, 1971), chap. 7.

33Paul Jewett, *Man as Male and Female* (Grand Rapids: Eerdmans, 1975).

Chapter Four: Furthering the Kingdom in Psychology

1From a poem by Archibald MacLeish, quoted in B. F. Skinner, *Cumulative Record: A Selection of Papers*, 3rd ed. (New York: Appleton-Century-Crofts, 1972), p. 351; first published in *The Boston Globe*, Oct. 9, 1971.

[2]Skinner, *Cumulative Record.*

[3]Holmes, *Contours of a World View.*

[4]Walter R. Thorson, "The Biblical Insights of Michael Polanyi," *Journal of the American Scientific Affiliation* 33 (1981):135.

[5]Wolterstorff, *Reason Within the Bounds of Religion.*

[6]Ibid., pp. 129-38.

[7]Holmes, *Contours of a World View.*

[8]C. Stephen Evans, *Preserving the Person: A Look at the Human Sciences* (Grand Rapids: Baker, 1982).

[9]John Donne, *Devotions upon Emergent Occasions* (Ann Arbor, Mich.: University of Michigan Press, 1960), pp. 108-9.

[10]John V. Taylor, *Enough Is Enough: A Biblical Call for Moderation in a Consumer-Oriented Society* (Minneapolis: Augsburg, 1977), p. 41.

[11]Ibid., p. 42.

[12]Evans, *Preserving the Person,* p. 144.

[13]Holmes, *Contours of a World-View,* p. 117.

[14]A modernization of an old Cornish prayer, quoted in Hendrik Berkhof, *Christ and the Powers,* trans. John H. Yoder (Scottdale, Pa.: Herald, 1977), p. 79.

[15]Michael A. Wallach and Lise Wallach, *Psychology's Sanction for Selfishness: The Error of Egoism in Theory and Therapy* (San Francisco: W. H. Freeman, 1983).

[16]Ibid., pp. 18-19.

[17]William K. Kilpatrick, *Psychological Seduction: The Failure of Modern Psychology* (Nashville: Nelson, 1983), p. 31.

[18]Wallach and Wallach, *Psychology's Sanction for Selfishness,* p. 21.

[19]Ibid., p. 181.

[20]Albert Bandura, *Social Learning Theory* (Englewood Cliffs, N.J.: Prentice-Hall, 1977).

[21]Howard Muson, "Moral Thinking: Can It Be Taught?" *Psychology Today* 12, no. 9 (1979):48-68, 92.

[22]Nicholas Wolterstorff, *Educating for Responsible Action* (Grand Rapids: Eerdmans, 1980).

[23]Al Dueck, "Religion and Morality: An Evaluation of Kohlberg's Theory of Moral Development" (Paper presented at the Christian Association for Psychological Studies Convention, Minneapolis, April 1979), p. 30.

[24]Kilpatrick, *Psychological Seduction,* p. 112.

[25]Ibid., pp. 114-15.

[26]Evans, *Preserving the Person,* p. 14.

[27]Harry F. Harlow, Margaret K. Harlow & Stephen J. Suomi, "From Thought to Therapy: Lessons from a Primate Laboratory," *American Scientist* 59 (1971):538-49.

[28]Ibid., p. 546.

[29]See Russell L. Mixter, ed., *Evolution and Christian Thought Today,* 2nd ed. (Grand Rapids: Eerdmans, 1960); Carl F. H. Henry, ed., *Horizons of Science: Christian Scholars Speak Out* (New York: Harper & Row, 1978).

30Dan Goleman, "A Conversation with Ulric Neisser," *Psychology Today* 17, no. 5 (1983):62.

31Chris Argyris, "Some Unintended Consequences of Rigorous Research," *Psychological Bulletin* 70 (1968):185.

32Ibid., p. 186.

33Zick Rubin, "Taking Deception for Granted," *Psychology Today* 17, no. 3 (1983):74-75.

34Kirk E. Farnsworth, *Integrating Psychology and Theology: Elbows Together but Hearts Apart* (Washington, D.C.: University Press of America, 1981); Mary Stewart Van Leeuwen, *The Sorcerer's Apprentice: A Christian Looks at the Changing Face of Psychology* (Downers Grove, Ill.: InterVarsity Press, 1982).

35Mark P. Cosgrove, *B. F. Skinner's Behaviorism: An Analysis* (Grand Rapids: Zondervan, 1982); Malcolm A. Jeeves, *Psychology and Christianity: The View Both Ways* (Downers Grove, Ill.: InterVarsity Press, 1976); David G. Myers, *The Human Puzzle: Psychological Research and Christian Belief* (San Francisco: Harper & Row, 1978); David G. Myers, *The Inflated Self: Human Illusions and the Biblical Call to Hope* (New York: Seabury, 1981); Thomas E. Ludwig, Merold Westphal, Robin J. Klay, & David G. Myers, *Inflation, Poortalk and the Gospel* (Valley Forge, Pa.: Judson, 1981); Martin Bolt & David G. Myers, *The Human Connection: How People Change People* (Downers Grove, Ill.: InterVarsity Press, 1984).

36Aleksandr I. Solzhenitsyn, *A World Split Apart: Commencement Address Delivered at Harvard University, June 8, 1978*, trans. Irina Ilovayskaya Alberti (New York: Harper & Row, 1978), pp. 17-19.

37Kirk E. Farnsworth, "Christian Psychotherapy and the Culture of Professionalism," *Journal of Psychology and Theology* 8 (1980):115-21.

38Kirk E. Farnsworth and W. H. Lawhead, *Life Planning: A Christian Approach to Careers* (Downers Grove, Ill.: InterVarsity Press, 1981).

Chapter Five: The Creative Arts

1H. Richard Niebuhr, *The Responsible Self* (New York: Harper & Row, 1963), pp. 151-52, 161.

2Michael Polanyi's way of saying this is that "we can know more than we can tell" (*The Tacit Dimension* [Garden City, N.Y.: Doubleday, 1966], p. 4).

3Flannery O'Connor, *Mystery and Manners,* eds. Sally and Robert Fitzgerald (New York: Farrar, Straus & Giroux, 1961), p. 73.

4Pablo Picasso, *The Arts,* May 1923.

5Quoted in Charles Kaplan, ed., *Criticism: The Major Statements* (New York: St. Martin's Press, 1975), p. 264.

6The best discussions are by Gene Edward Veith, Jr., *The Gift of Art* (Downers Grove, Ill.: InterVarsity Press, 1983); and Francis A. Schaeffer, *Art and the Bible* (Downers Grove: InterVarsity Press, 1974).

7Schaeffer, *Art and the Bible,* p. 61.

8Oscar Wilde, "The Decay of Lying," as reprinted in *The Modern Tradition: Backgrounds of Modern Literature,* eds. Richard Ellmann and Charles Feidelson, Jr. (New York: Oxford University Press, 1965), p. 20.

9Auriel Kolna, "Contrasting the Ethical with the Aesthetical," *British Journal of Aesthetics* 12 (1972):340. Although the word *beauty* has fallen out of vogue in scholarly circles, partly because it is inappropriate to modern art whose subject is ugliness, I am unwilling to relinquish the term for the simple reason that I have found again and again that it is the term with which ordinary people resonate. Whatever synonym we might choose, we obviously need some term by which to denote the technical excellence that we admire in an artistic composition. That the term *beauty* can continue to serve this function has been argued by Guy Sircello, *A New Theory of Beauty* (Princeton, N.J.: Princeton University Press, 1975).

10Gerard Manley Hopkins, "Poetry and Verse," as quoted in *Gerard Manley Hopkins: The Major Poems,* ed. Walford Davies (London: J. M. Dent and Sons, 1979), p. 38.

11Dorothy L. Sayers, *The Mind of the Maker* (1941; reprint ed., Cleveland: World Publishing, 1956), p. 34.

12Abraham Kuyper, *Calvinism* (Grand Rapids: Eerdmans, 1943), pp. 142, 156-57.

13H. R. Rookmaaker, *Art Needs No Justification* (Downers Grove: InterVarsity Press, 1978), pp. 38-39.

14C. S. Lewis, *Christian Reflections* (Grand Rapids: Eerdmans, 1967), p. 10.

15From the preface of Joseph Conrad, *The Nigger of the Narcissus* (New York: Collier Books, 1962), p. 19.

16O'Connor, *Mystery and Manners,* p. 84.

17Quoted by Virginia Stem Owens in *The Christian Imagination,* ed. Leland Ryken (Grand Rapids: Baker, 1981), p. 380.

18O'Connor, *Mystery and Manners,* p. 75.

19Jonathan Culler, *Structuralist Poetics: Structuralism, Linguistics, and the Study of Literature* (Ithaca, N.Y.: Cornell University Press, 1975), p. 115.

20See Schaeffer, *Art and the Bible,* pp. 56-59.

21T. S. Eliot, "Religion and Literature," reprinted in *The Christian Imagination,* ed. Ryken, pp. 142, 153.

22The passages include Acts 17:28; 1 Cor 15:33; and Titus 1:12. For commentary on the importance of this data for aesthetic theory, see my book *Triumphs of the Imagination: Literature in Christian Perspective* (Downers Grove, Ill.: InterVarsity Press, 1979), pp. 161-63.

23See Veith, *The Gift of Art,* pp. 57-58, for the details.

24John Calvin, *Commentaries on the Epistles to Timothy, Titus, and Philemon,* trans. William Pringle (Grand Rapids: Eerdmans, 1948), pp. 300-301.

Contributing Authors

Arthur F. Holmes (Ph.D., Northwestern) is a professor and department chairman of philosophy at Wheaton College, where he has taught since 1951. The author of several books, including *All Truth Is God's Truth* and *Contours of a World View*, he also wrote the "Christian Philosophy" article for *Encyclopaedia Britannica* (15th ed.), as well as numerous articles in professional and religious periodicals.

Mark A. Noll (Ph.D., Vanderbilt) is a professor of history and church history at Wheaton College, where he has taught since 1979. He is the author of *Christians in the American Revolution* (Eerdmans, 1977), and an editor of *The Bible in America* (Oxford, 1982) and *Eerdmans' Handbook to Christianity in America* (1983). His articles have appeared in professional journals and in Christian magazines like *HIS*, *Eternity* and *Christianity Today*. Prof. Noll is an editor of *The Reformed Journal*.

Joseph Spradley began teaching physics at Wheaton College in 1959 after completing the B.S., M.S. and Ph.D. at U.C.L.A. in engineering physics and four years of microwave antenna research at Hughes Aircraft Company. He took additional courses at Fuller Seminary, the Oak Ridge Institute of Nuclear Studies and in the history of science at the University of Oklahoma. He spent 1965-68 at Haigazian College in Beirut, Lebanon, including two years as acting president. During 1970-72 he served as senior lecturer and USAID science specialist at Ahmadu Bello University in Zaria, Nigeria.

Kirk Farnsworth (Ph.D., Iowa State) was a counseling psychologist and associate professor at the University of New Hampshire from 1968-75, and director of counseling and professor at Trinity College, Illinois, from 1975-83. He is currently a professor of psychology at Wheaton College. He is the author of *Integrating Psychology and Theology* and *Life Planning* (with Wendall H. Lawhead), and numerous articles in professional journals and Christian periodicals.

Leland Ryken has taught in the English Department at Wheaton College since 1968. He holds the Ph.D. from the University of Oregon. He is the author of articles and books on the poetry of John Milton, the Bible as literature, Renaissance literature, literary theory and Puritanism. His books on literary theory include *Triumphs of the Imagination: Literature in Christian Perspective* and *The Christian Imagination: Essays on Literature and the Arts*.